The Management of Independent Learning

EDITED BY

JO TAIT
PETER KNIGHT

KOGAN PAGE

Published in association with the
Staff and Educational Development Association

First published in 1996

Kogan Page Limited
120 Pentonville Road
London N1 9JN

British Library Cataloguing in Publication Data

A CIP record for this book is available from the British Library.

ISBN 0 7494 1949 0

Typeset by Kogan Page
Printed and bound in Great Britain by Clays Ltd, St Ives plc

Contents

Acknowledgements

Thanks are due to John Wakeford of the Unit for Innovation in Higher Education at Lancaster University for his unfailing support and encouragement. And for his vision. Also to Frank Wareing of the same unit for his poised, practical help.

Lee Harvey of the University of Central England, Bill Johnston of the Manchester Metropolitan University and Dave O'Reilly of the University of East London were all instrumental at the planning stage. Our thanks to them for their insight and encouragement.

David Boud has supported this project and encouraged us to make these papers widely known.

Jo Tait and
Peter Knight
Lancaster

Notes on contributors

Sue Bloxham is Director of Initial Youth and Community Work Training at the University College of St Martin, Lancaster. Her recent research activity includes action research studies of student learning in both college-based and fieldwork-based contexts, and an evaluative study of inter-agency collaboration in the field of young people's sexual health.

David Boud is Professor of Adult Education at the University of Technology, Sydney. He has been involved in innovative practices in teaching, learning and assessment in higher education over many years. His most recent books are: *Using Experience for Learning, Enhancing Learning through Self-assessment* and *Learning Contracts: A practical guide.*

Richard Carter is Professor of Electronic Engineering and Director of the Professional Development Unit in the School of Engineering, Computing and Mathematical Sciences at Lancaster University. He has taken a particular interest in aspects of teaching and learning, especially experiential learning and its application to education based in the workplace.

Frank Cooke made his first career in the Royal Air Force, moving into work in the engineering industry where he became a training manager. He currently works as an external consultant in training and human resource development and has close links with the Professional Development Unit of Lancaster University's School of Engineering, Computing and Mathematical Sciences.

Gordon Doughty took an eclectic Open University degree while working in the optical industry, then joined Glasgow University's Engineering Faculty for opto-electronics research and a PhD. He is now a senior lecturer organizing the BTechEd degree, the Robert Clark Centre for Technological Education, and collaborative projects on learning technologies.

Noel Entwistle is Bell Professor of Education and Director of the Centre for Research on Learning and Instruction at the University of Edinburgh. Current research involves the nature of academic understanding and the development of hypertext-based advice on study skills. He currently edits the journal, *Higher Education.*

Steve Ferguson's interest in the education of professionals is based upon many years' experience in teacher education, at both initial teacher education and continuing professional development levels. He is a member of the team funded by the Higher Education Funding Council for England to develop syndicate group methods in professional courses at the University of Liverpool where he is based.

Richard Freeman has worked in developing and running open and distance learning schemes since 1972. He now works as a freelance consultant in open learning, specializing in the development of learning materials and open learning courses. One of his most recent publications is *Quality Assurance in Training and Education* 1993, published by Kogan Page.

Peter Funnell is Dean of Cross-College Programmes and chair of the Teaching and Learning Methods Committee at the Suffolk College, Ipswich, and has institutional responsibility for learning resources and CATs developments. His research interests include the interface between humanistic educational practice and the developing entrepreneurial culture within UK post-compulsory education. He is joint series editor of the 'New Developments in Vocational Education' series of books (Kogan Page) and has contributed to a range of professional journals and other publications.

Phil Garrigan has worked extensively on the development of student profiles. A former teacher, now a teacher educator and coordinator for mentor training and support, her particular interest is in the assessment of professionals' autonomous learning.

Sharon Goddard is Deputy Head of the School of Humanities at the Suffolk College, Ipswich. She has responsibility for a range of curriculum initiatives in the fields of cultural and critical studies, media and literary studies, as well as contributing to research and practice in the areas of teaching and learning resources, staff development and course review and evaluation. Her research interests include issues in negotiated learning in higher education. She has contributed to the text, *Essential Research Skills* (Collins Educational, 1995).

Professor Lee Harvey is head of the Centre for Research into Quality at the University of Central England in Birmingham, and editor of the journal, *Quality in Higher Education*. With Peter Knight, he wrote *Transforming Higher Education*, published in 1996 by the Open University Press.

Mike Heathfield is a senior lecturer in Youth and Community Studies at the University College of St Martin, Lancaster. He is course leader for the postgraduate certificate course and has responsibility for placement quality issues within the department. His doctoral research examines the measurement of quality of professional placement performance in Youth and Community Work Training.

Patrick Hynes is a research associate in the Department of Educational Research at Lancaster University. He has taught at a range of levels, from school through to undergraduate and Masters level. His research interests include the evaluation of computer-based learning, the future development of Internet-based learning resources, and the use of Computer Mediated Communication to support teaching and learning.

William Johnston is course leader for the BA(Hons) degree course in independent study at the Manchester Metropolitan University. He is Director in European Cultural and Social Studies at the universities of Helsinki, Joensuu, Lapland, Tromso, Amsterdam, Madrid and Athens, and coordinator of the Arctic Studies Programme at the University of Lapland. He edits the *International Journal for Independent Studies*.

Peter Knight is a lecturer in the Department of Educational Research at Lancaster University. He has a range of teaching and research interests, focusing both on the school sector and post-compulsory education, on which topics he has edited or written a dozen books and many more articles.

Hazel Knox, initially education guidance adviser, is now the Deputy Director of the Centre for CATs and Continuing Education at the University of Paisley. She is course leader for approximately 2,000 students enrolled on CATs and has carried out research into how students perform on flexible programmes of study.

Selena Mason is currently the education research officer at Middlesex University Students' Union. Her research interests include systems of student representation and feedback. Previously Selena worked on the Quality in Higher Education project at the University of Central England.

Bob Neal is a qualified engineer who has worked for the BBC in a number of fields, spanning engineering, personnel training and project management. He has worked as a director and as a consultant for the Alvey directorate of the Department of Trade and Industry. He is now a senior teaching Fellow in the School of Engineering, Computing and Mathematical Sciences at Lancaster University.

Jane Pearce, formerly coordinator of the Flexible Learning Initiatives Project at the University of Liverpool, is now living in Perth, Western Australia, and working as an educational consultant.

Suzanne Robertson was formerly principal lecturer and teaching and learning coordinator in the School of Health Studies at the University of Sunderland. She is currently manager of learning development services with responsibility for introducing innovations and development in learning into the core teaching activities across the University of Sunderland.

Christine Steeples is a research associate and is director of Lancaster's Advanced Learning Technology Programme. Her research investigates key characteristics of success in using Computer Mediated Communication to support collaborative learning. She has interests in the use of multimedia in collaborative learning environments, particularly the use of stored voice annotations.

Ron Stewart has taught courses in the psychology of education for many years, and currently has overall responsibility for the modular MEd at Liverpool University. He is also the evaluator on the HEFCE-funded Flexible Learning Project, which has been set up to support innovation in teaching and learning in other parts of the university.

Jo Tait is a recent mature graduate in Independent Studies at Lancaster and currently works as a training officer in staff development at the same institution. Her personal enthusiasms centre on the inherent value of lifelong learning processes to the individual.

Professor Michael Thorne is currently Pro Vice-Chancellor at the University of Sunderland, where his responsibilities are for learning and student support, recruitment, the Student Charter, and IT strategy. He is the author or co-author of 11 books and a number of academic papers and articles.

Karen Valley is a lecturer in advanced learning technology, and is deputy director of Lancaster's Advanced Learning Technology Programme. The main focus of her research is the design, implementation and use of software for education and training. Her interests include Computer Mediated Communication-supported learning, the educational use of the Internet, cognitive psychology, and knowledge-based systems.

Chapter 1

A framework

Jo Tait and Peter Knight

INDEPENDENT LEARNING AND INDEPENDENT STUDIES

There is growing interest in government and amongst industrialists and academics in the development of key competences through higher education programmes. The National Goals for Education are a North American manifestation of a trend that is represented in the UK by the development of NVQs, SVQs and GNVQs. Central to this book is the idea that there is much to be gained by independent, flexible or open learning. Following the idea that people able to thrive in the twenty-first century will have to be lifelong learners, and embracing the notion that skilled, self-motivated people with initiative are likely to be the greatest asset of Western nations, we identify the development of the capability to work autonomously as a key competence to be fostered by the education system.

There has been little systematic treatment of how key competences might be developed, let alone of the implications of trying to do so. This book, by focusing on the competences associated with self-motivated lifelong learners who are accustomed to working with autonomy, provides models for exploring ways to develop competences in a changing world. Drawing upon analyses and case studies from England, Scotland and Australasia, it examines a variety of issues, setting them in the context of accounts of emerging practices. Particular attention is given to the promise of information technology in supporting and fostering independent learning, recognizing the growing prospect that in the twenty-first century the 'virtual university' may be commonplace.

OPEN/SELF-DIRECTED/FLEXIBLE LEARNING AND INDEPENDENT STUDY

These approaches have attracted widespread interest, holding out the promise of easier access to higher education for groups that have been excluded because of domestic and personal circumstances. It has also been said that there are advantages to institutions in making it possible for learners to work at their own pace, in their own times. Flexible learning is a way of putting the learner in control of the learning and as such has affinities with Independent Studies (IS). However, the term covers a multitude of practices: 'this area of education is notorious for its inability to pin down the particularities of open/flexible/self-directed/student-centred/resource-based and assorted other less traditional forms of learning' (Telford, 1995, p.165). It might be helpful to argue that flexible learning methods may be plotted on a continuum, as shown in Figure 1.1.

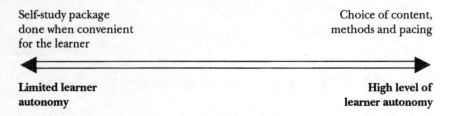

Self-study package done when convenient for the learner

Choice of content, methods and pacing

Limited learner autonomy

High level of learner autonomy

Figure 1.1 *A continuum of flexible learning strategies*

So, a self-study pack, where the content is prescribed by the degree programme and where the methods of enquiry are constrained by the format of the pack, would lie towards the left of the continuum, exhibiting a high level of control over the student's learning. Flexible learning strategies, especially where they are print-based, convergent and 'writerly', can themselves work in favour of people with what could loosely be called 'cultural capital', despite the ostensible aim of improving access to higher education for marginalized groups. Such strategies may give learners some control over *when* they learn but at the expense of organizational approaches (course readers, workbooks, and work-based learning centred on management's agenda, for example) that may serve to close down *what* they learn.

In contrast, dissertation-style approaches to flexible learning would lie more to the right of the continuum, since learners would have more control over the choice of topic and, sometimes, over the choice of methods of enquiry. Where learners also set the goals of learning, then the work would lie even further to the right.

Independent study or autonomous learning can also be classified on the continuum used for flexible learning, but when talking about IS a more complex model is needed. Figure 1.2 suggests that Independent Studies can be classified according to the level of autonomy that the learners have, as with flexible learning, and according to the extent to which independent study characterizes a programme. The arrow points away from tokenistic and unsatisfactory dabblings with the notion of IS (see Chapter 3), towards programmes that have the potential to deliver the benefits described in this chapter and throughout the book. Many things may be called IS but only those that lie towards the bottom right quadrant deserve the name.

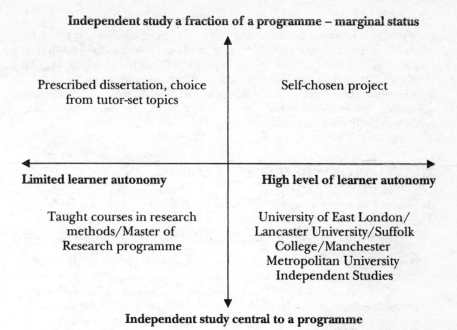

Independent study a fraction of a programme – marginal status

Prescribed dissertation, choice from tutor-set topics

Self-chosen project

Limited learner autonomy

High level of learner autonomy

Taught courses in research methods/Master of Research programme

University of East London/ Lancaster University/Suffolk College/Manchester Metropolitan University Independent Studies

Independent study central to a programme

Figure 1.2 *A typology of IS courses*

The greatest benefits are available where programmes are designed to lead the learner towards independence (it does not necessarily come naturally) and to allow learners to reach the stage where they choose and formulate the problems for study, as well as the methods of enquiry and, to some degree within the regulations for degree classification, the criteria of appreciation as well. Funnell and Goddard describe the development of a model of this in Chapter 6. Such programmes are taken to be programmes of independent study. Thus, it is possible to have independent learning, which is something of value and utility but not to have the complete programme of IS. In order to get the most from independent learning, a programme needs to be based upon it – IS can maximize the promise of flexible, open or independent learning.

Bernstein (1975) analysed school curricula in terms of framing and classification. Framing refers to the degree to which a curriculum is structured for the learner. This is similar to the control-autonomy dimension that has been used above to classify flexible learning and IS programmes. Classification refers to the degree to which the curriculum is organized around separate knowledge categories, such as academic subjects. Most secondary school curricula are highly classified. It is possible to have flexible learning in highly classified higher education programmes, although IS programmes that lie in the bottom right quadrant of Figure 1.2 will not be highly classified, since the choice of content is under the control of the learner. But this weak classification also indicates a problem for IS programmes: academic subjects have symbolic importance. The danger is that IS programmes, because they do not necessarily induct learners into traditional bodies of knowledge, deprive learners of this symbolic cultural capital. Weak framing may be good for allowing learners to choose topics for understanding and to work in areas that interest them, but the penalty may be that they graduate without possessing the symbolic advantage of a degree in a known subject with established worth and standards.

THE VALUE OF INDEPENDENT LEARNING AND IS

Jo Tait, one of the authors of this chapter, obtained, as a mature student, a degree in IS at Lancaster. Her comments lead us to see that IS has benefits that outweigh the lack of a perceived disciplinary base:

> Previously I had worked in child-rearing, retail and catering in the 'real world', and in adult and further education for a brief period. Purely based on my own experience of IS, I feel that the process of studying in this environment was crucial in challenging my deep-rooted and limited ideas about my potential self-worth. In addition, I found that many of the 'normal' meanings and values of working life came under scrutiny. The IS process raised some personal and global questions about the purposes of higher education, research and learning itself and I'm glad to see these questions that still mean so much to me being discussed throughout this volume. I'm particularly interested in how far the transformative potential of IS depends upon the prior experiences and the degree of engagement of the individual student.

> I want to take up the claim that graduates in IS could feel disadvantaged in some job markets because they have not been encultured into a recognized area of study. Anecdotal evidence from peers and my experience of working since graduation lead me to believe that the reflective learning habits developed through independent study support the development and application of skills which outweigh the value of a specific knowledge base.

Harvey and Mason suggest in Chapter 2 that the practical value of a discipline or subject base may be exaggerated. The skills of value that IS can develop include:

- the ability to identify problems and work creatively towards solutions;
- the ability to reflect and build on knowledge as it is accumulated;
- skill in working with others and appreciation of the benefits of collaboration;

- a willingness to see and benefit from a learning opportunity wherever it presents itself;

- the ability to take a risk and *do*, not just to plan;

- an ability to continue to learn from learning.

These are precisely the type of skills, competences or practices valued by employers and by those who see higher education as one part of the development of people committed to lifelong learning.

LEARNER AUTONOMY AND THE AIMS OF HIGHER EDUCATION

At this point there is no intention of considering the merits of the account-ability-driven view of the purposes of higher education. It is sufficient to note that, certainly at higher levels, UK government vocational qualifications, such as the National Vocational Qualifications (NVQs), the Scottish Vocational Qualifications (SVQs) and the General National Vocational Qualifications (GNVQs), value learner autonomy. Whatever reservations the academic community may have about these vocational qualifications (see Hyland, 1993, for example), they do not directly threaten the principle of developing learner autonomy, although in other ways they are considerably more prescriptive than IS programmes.

An alternative account of the value of higher education dwells on the intrinsic value of the processes of education: it does not have to be for anything – it is good of itself. This liberal view of learning is by no means antithetical to independent learning. Its goals might be characterized as a commitment to developing wisdom and a commitment to the notion of learning for life. Both are concepts that give primacy to the individual: as a person of wisdom and as a lifelong learner. This fits well with current thinking about the process of learning in higher education. As Biggs (1993) has insisted, learning is relational: it involves individuals in relating new information, concepts or processes to their existing webs of knowledge and understanding. Inevitably, this is both a communal and an individual process. It is communal in the sense that individuals are members of a culture, sharing a language, but it is individual in the sense that everyone has their own, distinct mental structures and understandings within the communal milieu. Learning, then, is to a marked degree an individual activity and the concept of liberal learning places considerable emphasis on the development of the individual. It is hard to see how this position can be simply reconciled with directive, didactic models of education.

Traditionally, higher education has been judged on the degree to which learners have mastered and understood a body of knowledge and proce-dures. However, employers seem to value certain personal qualities. Little work has been done on how these might be promoted within higher education. However, a piece of American research is of interest in that context. Pascarella *et al.* (1994) investigated the correlates of learning for self-understanding and found that, particularly for women, the level of social interaction related positively to levels of self-understanding. Now, if an aim of education is to promote certain personal qualities, it might be claimed that this entails increased self-understanding on the part of the learners – it amounts to a form of social metacognition that is enhanced, according to Pascarella and colleagues, by social interaction. It is hard to see how traditional higher education programmes foster such interaction, let alone do so with key competences in mind. That is not to say that IS and flexible learning will necessarily do so. The phrase 'independent learning' is redolent of the solitary student. However, this resonance may be misleading. The independence lies in choice: choice of topic and choice of methods of enquiry. As Johnston makes clear (Chapter 14), group work can be intimately associated with independent studies programmes. At Lancaster, it has been a cardinal feature of first-year work and some students continue to work in groups at later stages of their programme. There are, of course, many forms of flexible learning and independent study, varying with the stage at which the learners are (Knight, Chapter 3; Carter, Cooke and Neal, Chapter 7) and with the institutional context (see, for example, Doughty, Chapter 9; Bloxham and Heathfield, Chapter 5; Knox, Chapter 4). But because of the flexibility that independent study allows, it is not only possible for learners to choose topics that enhance their self-understanding (as I [JT] did when investigating the Alexander Technique in my IS degree); to use methods that help understanding (by, for example, showing the learner that he or she is not good at making a start on a task, possibly for fear of failure); but it also lends itself to collaborative work, which provides the social interaction that has been associated with better learning (Perret-Clermont, 1980) and, by Pascarella and colleagues (1994), with greater self-understanding.

The claim needs to be put carefully. It is not that learners understand themselves better and hence are more disposed to show those personal qualities that employers – and others – value. It is that IS has goals and organizational characteristics that make it easier for that to happen than is the case in the traditional, didactic programme. There is, then, a sense in which IS can be seen to develop the whole person rather than simply fattening the mind. Interestingly, Boud (in Chapter 11) suggests that the field of adult education traditionally espouses these goals and provides the ideal environment for practical application of those principles.

IS AND HOLISTIC LEARNING

What this implies is that with IS we are understanding learning as something that is holistic, as more than just exercise for cognition. Jo continues,

This holistic learning was certainly a prominent feature of my time as an IS student. One part of my degree involved evaluating the new (in 1990) first-year module in IS at Lancaster, which I had just completed. The qualitative research I undertook was both strengthened and sabotaged (in terms of objectivity) by my own involvement and participation with my peers and the fact that the 'client' for any outcomes was the tutor group who were still working to perfect the programme. In order that the project might serve a practical purpose and as the result of discussion with tutors, students and supervisor, I decided not to write an analysis of many interviews in the form of a report as we had originally planned. Instead, I chose to develop an interactive board and role play game which aimed to unpack and explore the often challenging group and project work which was, at that time, the essential core of Lancaster's first-year IS programme.

The process of renegotiation concerning assessment and learning outcomes took place in many of my IS modules and, I think, contributed enormously to many of the positive outcomes I have identified as possible in an IS learning environment. Perhaps I should make it clear that the IS degree at Lancaster does not invite students to 'make it up as they go along'. Each prospective student, at the beginning of the course, submits a proposal which states learning outcomes for each unit and provides an indication of coherence for the whole programme. This principle has undoubted value to students, supervisors and assessors. However, my experience was that supervisors and administrators seemed willing to delay final closure on the outcomes and criteria by which my work was assessed. The positive result of this open-ended attitude was that the IS Part One programme had a usable product. In addition, as a student I was able to reflect on the learning process itself [see also Knight, Chapter 3 and Entwistle, Chapter 10] and benefited greatly from the experience of negotiating the criteria for assessment based on the actual outcomes.

Chapters 4–8, 12 and 14 in this volume show how other learners have responded to other flexible approaches offered by other institutions and Boud, in Chapter 11, stresses the advantages of developing an educational culture that openly and positively values negotiated learning.

Knight (1995) refers to the risks in over-defining the outcomes of learning in higher education, reducing opportunities for creativity or freshness; for fruitful mistakes and for exploring dead ends. In the IS framework, maintaining openness about outcomes until the last possible moment can both enrich the learning and enhance the value of the final outcome. It also corresponds more closely with the optimum working environment of many successful graduates, in which problems – and their solutions – are frequently fuzzy and unstructured, as Jo's commentary suggests:

I have said that it was not at all clear, at the beginning of my programme of IS, that renegotiation was permitted. There were many difficulties associated with being able to form the assessment in order to frame the real requirements of the work in hand. The personal process transformed me from a reactive or strategic student [see Noel Entwistle, Chapter 10] to a deeply engaged learner, participating in my own learning for my own purposes. The research and presentation methods as well as the content of each assignment were considered, significant and personalized. At all stages, I took risks which challenged the established systems and courted failure but the final transformation took place when I realized that, whether or not I graduated, I was achieving my own objectives. This Commitment [*sic*, Perry, 1970] has since proved its value in many work and interview situations.

IS AND LIFELONG LEARNING

It is hard to see how such learning might be generally fostered by higher education unless learners have the experience of some true independent study in a supportive IS learning environment. The added value of the autonomous nature of the model graduate is that she or he should *continue* to apply the principles of learning gained from higher education in a variety of circumstances.

This graduate should be able to manage change effectively, especially in the turbulent circumstances of modern times (Peters, 1992). As Alvin Toffler said:

> The illiterate of the year 2000 will not be the individual who cannot read and write, but the one who cannot learn, unlearn and relearn. (Toffler, cit. Gelb and Buzan, 1994, p.83)

Moreover, argue Harvey and Mason (1995), the graduate who has the potential to transform organizations, who may bring about fundamental change in some part of their activity, is the graduate who is especially prized.

PEDAGOGY AND IS

Unless higher education is to be regarded as nothing more than a rite of passage, as was the case in the ancient universities of England in the eighteenth century, then whatever the goals of higher education, there are questions to be asked about the pedagogy. Yet here too there is a happy convergence with learner autonomy. In Chapter 10, Noel Entwistle provides a succinct summary of research into learning in higher education. Independent learning has been associated with better learning, principally because it is congenial to the deep approaches to learning that are seen to be both desirable in their own right and to be the most efficient ways of learning for understanding.[1]

However, good learning depends on dispositions and motivation. How can higher education motivate learners to adopt deep approaches, rather than to take the easy route of surface learning? To some degree, it is limited in what it can do. There is a host of factors – finance, hormones, families, music and the temptations of what is for many the first taste of independent living – that affect learners' motivation and about which universities can do little. There are also the expectations learners bring with them that affect what they are willing to see as learning and that shape their ways of working. However, these expectations appear to be malleable, as long as institutions of higher education take care to convey clearly to learners the purposes and significance of what they are doing. Here, it is important that the ways in which student learning are assessed reinforce the claims of learning programmes, rather than undermine them: traditional assessment systems can tend to encourage surface learning (see Chapters 10 and 11). Yet assessment reform and addressing students' concerns and interests are not, of themselves, sufficient to sustain a motivation for deep learning. As Entwistle and Ramsden (1983) observed, a certain learning environment is needed: one in which there is not a workload that inhibits enquiries in depth (see also Chapter 5) and where students can exercise choice. This is consistent with a review of the North American literature by Pascarella and Terenzini (1991; see also Chapter 15). IS programmes are marked by such features and independent learning courses may be, especially where the flexibility of computer-assisted learning is brought to bear.

This pedagogy also offers benefits to university managers, who are faced in all developed countries with the problem of educating more students, of educating a more diverse student population with units of resource that are at best static, at worst declining. The promise of independent learning is that where students are inducted into the culture of autonomy from the beginning (see Chapters 3 and 6), then they can, by the closing stages of their programme, work without making such heavy demands on staff time as is the case with traditional curriculum 'delivery'. Three chapters in this book: Chapters 8 and 9 (on the use of advanced learning technologies) and 12 (on the virtual university), explore ways in which modern technology can further support and enhance learner autonomy with potential savings in staff time. Some caution is needed here, since many approaches to enhancing learner autonomy can involve a lot of one-to-one tutor–student contact, or involve tutors supervising lots of small groups. This can be considerably more expensive than traditional teaching methods. Similarly, flexible learning that is dependent on the production of specialist materials can be expensive and hard to do well. And all development in the use of technology (and, of course, all curriculum change) is subject to the necessity for a considerable and skilful staff development programme, as noted in Chapters 12 and 13. Yet, with foresight, there is a possibility of a curriculum based on the goal of promoting learner autonomy leading to some savings in staff time.

THE ORGANIZATION OF IS AND OF INDEPENDENT LEARNING

It's scary being an independent learner. Doyle (1983), analysing school classrooms, argued that children seek to reduce risk and to minimize ambiguity so that they then know exactly what to do in order to get good grades. Likewise, Galton and Williamson (1992) observed children's discomfort with group work, where they expected the teacher to define the task and the solution strategy for them. University students are older and have greater academic achievements but we can recognize similar traits amongst them.

Jo is able to describe her own anxieties and those of her fellow students while they were engaging with IS at Lancaster:

> There were many times when we envied those students who were taking 'normal' courses where the course itself defined the work that was expected and the standards against which it would be measured. My own experience of 'a reflection upon a reflection upon the learning process' is recorded in the final assignment of my degree from which the above quotation is taken. In this very reflective project, I abandoned all attempts to distinguish between academic objectivity and personal subjectivity. I was fortunate in my supervisors who assured me that it was 'normal' to feel overwhelmed and inadequate at certain stages of an inquiry. I was also directed to a book that suggested, '...you may be as soaring and psychotic and as specific and obsessional as you wish, so that you may explore the relationship between [personal experience and objective research]' (Bannister in Reason and Rowan, 1982, p.199). It seemed I might even need to risk insanity, letting go of all previously safe and fixed ideas, in the search for the truly rewarding learning state. The quality of supervision and support allowed the learning process to be engagingly dangerous. Although not all IS students were prepared to go to these lengths, I know that I was not the only student to experience heightened states of anxiety and pleasure while learning. Those who were prepared to take those risks tended to achieve a higher class of degree in the final assessment.

This discussion about risk, commitment and personal engagement raises an important question: is the first prerequisite for achieving autonomy as a learner simply dispositional? Do students need to come with a willingness to take risks and with the self-esteem sufficient to bear that risk? Ideally, these learners would have had positive previous experiences in schools (which are also expected to stimulate autonomous learning) but it is often found that the business of preparing 18-year-olds for the UK 'A' level examinations has had the opposite effects. Mature students seem to be more attracted to independent study than standard entry students (see Chapters 5 and 11) but the fear of failure is often more deeply rooted in the student who has not entered university by the 'normal' route. A mature student may have acknowledged the value of his or her own life experience, and even have gained admittance to higher education based on accreditation of that value. The leap of confidence required in daring to apply that experience to designing and carrying out an academic project is of another order of magnitude. Add to this the cultural confusion of multiple assessment criteria within many institutions (as contrasted with the coherent system described by Boud in Chapter 11) and the personal challenges associated with the deep learning process, and we should not be surprised that students may resist the risk-taking, innovative thinking highly valued in industry and associated with first-class honours in most degree programmes.

This does not lead to the conclusion that only those who are already robust risk-takers can grow into autonomy. Rather it suggests that many students will need:

- reassurance

- support

- academic guidance

- induction into the methods and habits of independent learning, and

- plenty of useful, formative feedback.

The paradox is that in order to become readier to be independent learners, many students will need a structure in the first place. Such heresy is quite compatible with the writing of Vygotsky, for example, on the process of learning. Lancaster's first-year IS programme is increasingly structured in response to the outcomes of research (see Chapter 3) so as to help students new to the ideas of IS achieve the skills and confidence they will require at higher levels. Funnell and Goddard (Chapter 6) describe similar modifications made to the Suffolk programme in response to experience.

An advantage that IS has over more constrained programmes is that it is possible to do this through work on topics that matter to the learners and that capitalize on what a student brings. Maturity and a 'real-life' context are undoubted advantages for successful IS programmes. The programmes described by Boud (Chapter 11) and Carter, Cooke and Neal (Chapter 7) make personal and professional relevance a prerequisite and provide for systematic recognition of prior learning. While work-based learning and APL provide some undoubted advantages for the learner, we have described above the elements of support that could lead students to take full advantage of IS in their undergraduate learning programme. It is also clear that group projects can provide the learning environment in which 'real-world' experiences can challenge all students and contribute to the development of that confidence expected of graduates (Johnston, Chapter 14).

CONCLUSION

Like all ideals, autonomy in learning is not attainable by all. Nor is it easy to attain an ideal. However, that's no reason not to have the ideal!

The chapters which follow examine in detail elements of independent learning and IS and identify many practical and pedagogical obstacles to fulfilling its promise. In reading this volume, we hope that you will increase your understanding of the organizational elements of change, of the influence that technology and culture bring to bear on learning and of the ways in which students experience a range of flexible, open and independent learning situations. Most of all, we hope that you will find that, at the core of the book, there is an appreciation of the urgent need to improve each individual student's crucial competence to cope with this changing world. It seems to us that our willingness to examine our programmes of undergraduate study and to 'revise and revise again' (Boud, Chapter 11) demonstrates our own commitment to and passion for the development of reflective and autonomous graduates, both for their own benefit and for our own, as participants in the world we are creating.

NOTE

1. Readers are invited to nominate the most effective methods for learning without understanding. Any resemblance to prevalent university pedagogies may be purely coincidental.

Chapter 2

A quality graduate

Lee Harvey and Selena Mason

For many years, employers have been concerned about the ability of graduates to work in a modern organization. This concern pre-dates the recent rapid expansion in higher education and the concomitant concerns, expressed in some quarters, about the standards and abilities of graduates in the 1990s. The real issue is not whether graduates are better or worse in absolute terms than they were in previous decades. Rather, it is to do with the integration of new graduates into an organization and the speed at which they can contribute effectively that has become a critical factor.

There are several reasons for this interest in the definition of the qualities of the effective graduate. First, in a rapidly changing world there is less time for graduates to become acclimatized to a particular setting – increasingly graduates are expected to be able to 'hit the deck running'. Second, although many larger organizations train graduates, small and medium enterprises (SMEs) have less resources for training and expect a more rapid return on their investment in graduates. Third, the growth of the world market means that if Britain is to remain internationally competitive then graduates will need to be versatile and flexible as well as knowledgeable. Fourth, and more fundamental in the educational context, is the shift to addressing the student perspective and the consequent need to respond by empowering students for lifelong learning through enhancing a range of skills and abilities, as well as knowledge.

This chapter will outline what constitutes the abilities of effective graduates from the point of view of employers, drawing on wide-ranging research undertaken through the Quality in Higher Education (QHE) project (Harvey, 1993; Harvey with Green, 1994). That will be followed by an exploration of what independent study can contribute to the development of these abilities.

There is, of course, a basic question raised by any attempt to define a quality graduate, whether from the point of view of employers or of any other external stakeholder. Whose needs should higher education be attempting to fulfil? It may be legitimate to suggest that higher education rightly serves its own purposes or the requirements of students and that employers should not dictate the nature of the outcome – higher education is not, after all, a training institution for employers. However, as will be demonstrated, the question of what characterizes an effective graduate cannot be reduced to the notion that this is stepping on the road that leads to higher education providing employer-fodder!

WHY DO ORGANIZATIONS EMPLOY GRADUATES?

It is often taken for granted that organizations employ graduates because they want bright (CUCD, 1990) or brainy (Darby, 1993) people and because a degree not only identifies such people but also provides evidence that the graduate has learned something beyond native intelligence. The employment of intelligent people might be a reason for employing graduates in itself, but then why does not everybody attempt to employ graduates? It is important to go beyond the notion of intelligence or brains to try and identify what it is that a graduate has to offer by dint of being intelligent.

Several studies have provided lists of the advantages of employing graduates, describing graduates as demonstrating flexibility, ambition, logical thinking, quick learning, high levels of motivation, good communication skills, creativity, maturity, specialist knowledge, analytic skills, initiative, and so on (Gordon, 1983: NBEET, 1992).

The QHE research, based on empirical investigation and literature review, suggests that there are four underlying reasons for the employment of graduates:

- the knowledge and ideas graduates bring to an organization;
- their willingness to learn and speed of learning;
- their flexibility, adaptability and ability to deal with change;
- their logical, analytic, critical, problem-solving and synthetic skills and the impact they have on innovation.

Although there may be differing emphases, these reasons are common to both large and small firms.

The enhancement continuum

The four underlying reasons for employing graduates can be seen as lying on an enhancement continuum which ranges from adding to an organization at one end to transforming the organization at the other (see Figure 2.1). The more that graduate employees are able to operate along the continuum, the greater the potential evolution of the organization.

This is not, of course, to suggest that *only* graduates are able to contribute to the evolution of an organization. The model is suggested as a means of exploring the rationale for employing graduates and employer satisfaction with the graduates they recruit.

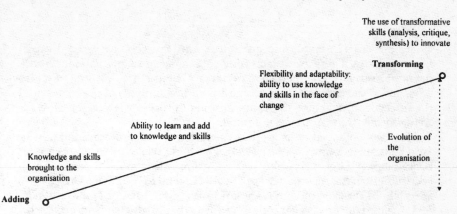

Figure 2.1 *The enhancement continuum*

Respondents in a study by Gordon (1983), mainly from large organizations, noted that graduates bring a fresh, creative mind to a job, are quick to learn, tend to question assumptions and are therefore more able to cope with change. In many cases they also bring to the job a level of specific technological knowledge. The earlier QHE study also suggested that employers are looking for more than just competent graduates who can do a job: what they really want are graduates who can make an impression on the way an organization functions (Harvey *et al.*, 1993).

Johnson *et al.* (1993, pp.92–4) found that half the small employers they interviewed confessed to a lack of awareness of what graduates might offer and said that, quite simply, they had never even considered employing a graduate. However, despite some employers having a highly pejorative view of the intelligence of graduates, SMEs which did employ them appreciated the alternative perspectives that graduates offered. A graduate, they often said, will come with an outsider's view, not one which has been coloured by experience of working here. So, said these respondents, graduates don't start off with preconceptions about what the answers might be. Over a quarter of the SMEs in their study saw graduates as potential generators of new and fresh ideas. Much empirical material (Harvey and Knight, 1996) reaffirms the thesis that, irrespective of size, organizations that recruit graduates are looking for *transformative potential*.

Employers are often criticized for not being clear about what they want from graduates. This imprecision is not surprising if employers are focusing on potential. By its very nature, transformative potential is elusive and dynamic. It is not a matter of specifying clear requirements for an unambiguous purpose, as if ordering stock from a supplier. Graduate recruitment thus has a speculative component that can only be hazily sketched, although it is clear that employers are looking for a suite of potentially transforming skills, attributes and attitudes.

In the following sections we will explore employer priorities and satisfaction in the light of the model proposed above.

Costs

There are costs in employing graduates, not least costs incurred through higher salaries. There are also training costs, since most graduates have little or no industrial or commercial experience. The training investment is also a risk given the career aspirations and potential mobility of graduates, and the uncertainty attaching to the appointment process when the employer is trying to spot transformative potential.

However, financial costs are not identified as a major consideration in larger organizations (Gordon, 1993). Graduate recruitment has been cut back in many large firms, but this is in line with a general reduction in recruitment in the recessionary period. SMEs tend to be much more circumspect about the cost of employing and training graduates (Johnson *et al.*, 1993). This concern is aggravated by a fear that graduates tend not to stay in SMEs and use them as a jumping-off point to bigger things. Forty-three per cent of Johnson *et al.*'s respondents were doubtful that their small company would be attractive to graduates at all.

In general and in principle, larger employers tend to see relatively few disadvantages in employing graduates, although, as we shall see, they might prefer that graduates were more accomplished in some respects. Indeed, larger employers overwhelmingly indicated that they thought graduates were more productive than other workers (Gordon, 1983, p.47). In any event, it is important for all employers to review their need for graduates and have a strategic plan that identifies how they will be used (DTI/CIHE, 1990).

Potentially, SMEs have a lot to gain from recruiting graduates who, through their knowledge, flexibility, innovativeness and day-to-day management skills, would enhance the effectiveness of the organization. SMEs have been seen as the engines for future economic regeneration and graduates are the fuel those engines might need. The further SMEs move along the continuum from viewing graduates as adding value to seeing them as vital to a transformative organization, the more appealing graduate recruitment is likely to become.

Furthermore, the increasing numbers of graduates and growing graduate unemployment are likely to lead to a reduction in the differential cost of employing a graduate. The notion of the graduate job and a predetermined career path progression for graduates is fast disappearing (Darby, 1993).

> Employees can no longer expect to retain discrete specialisms and predetermined career paths. The ability to transfer and combine skills and to influence the work process is assuming increasing importance. (BT, 1993, p.3)

This propitious set of circumstances provides SMEs with an opportunity for increasing the quality of their recruits. However, the potential benefits do not appear, at present, to outweigh the perceived disadvantages.

Furthermore, higher education careers officers need to raise graduate awareness about the potential of SMEs as a source of challenging and varied employment. Phillips-Kerr's (1991, p.7) sample of graduates, for example, identified variety of duties and interest as among the main criteria graduates apply in making career choices. Similarly, final-year students identified intellectual challenge and an opportunity to be creative and original as the two most important factors influencing their career choice.

WHAT DO EMPLOYERS WANT FROM GRADUATES?

Employers want graduates who not only add value but are likely to take the organization forward in the face of continuous and rapid change. Five broad areas of graduate attributes emerge from the research as being of major importance to employers:

- knowledge
- intellectual ability
- ability to work in a modern organization
- interpersonal skills
- communication.

Knowledge

Undergraduate education is frequently seen as developing students' knowledge. However, as much as this may be a useful context for developing many other skills and abilities, it is unusual – except in very limited areas – for a recruit from an undergraduate course to provide an organization with technical knowledge that might provide a market edge.

Table 2.1 *Employer importance ratings of graduate attributes*

Attribute	Mean	Rank
Willingness to learn	92.77	1
Commitment	88.29	2
Dependability/reliability	88.10	3
Self-motivation	87.81	4
Team work	87.40	5
Communication skills (oral)	86.89	6
Cooperation	85.83	7
Communication skills (written)	85.66	8
Drive/energy	84.52	9
Self-management	84.50	10
Desire to achieve/motivation	84.33	11

Attribute	Mean	Rank
Problem-solving ability	84.02	12
Analytic ability	82.99	13
Flexibility	82.94	14
Initiative	82.85	15
Can summarize key issues	82.47	16
Logical argument	82.28	17
Adaptability (intellectual)	81.35	18
Numeracy	80.99	19
Adaptability (organizational)	80.36	20
Can cope with pressure/stress	79.96	21
Time management	79.96	21
Rapid conceptualization of issues	79.33	23
Enquiry and research skills	79.10	24
Self-confidence	78.31	25
Persistence/tenacity	78.20	26
Planning ability	78.07	27
Interest in lifelong learning	77.29	28
Ability to use information technology	77.25	29
Understanding of core principles	76.98	30
Organizational skills	76.86	31
Critical ability	76.79	32
Can deal with large amounts of information	76.77	33
Consideration for others	76.45	34
Leadership potential	76.03	35
Independent judgement	76.02	36
Ability to relate to wider context	75.39	37
Maturity	75.00	38
Tact	74.79	39
Equipped for continuous education	74.58	40
Innovation	74.18	41
Loyalty	73.80	42
Tolerance	73.70	43
Technical ability	73.41	44
Influencing skills	73.14	45
Decision-making skills	72.95	46
Curiosity	71.63	47
Imagination	69.47	48
Creativity	67.83	49
Experience of the world of work	67.08	50
Leadership ability	66.32	51
Commercial awareness	66.04	52
General knowledge	65.55	53
Financial knowledge or understanding	64.18	54
Negotiation skills	62.60	55

Attribute	Mean	Rank
Deep understanding	61.71	56
Relevant work experience	57.29	57
Problem-setting ability	57.17	58
Specialist factual knowledge	55.20	59
Knowledge of social/political issues	49.21	60
Knowledge of the organization	47.52	61
Prior knowledge of the job	45.83	62

For some employers the subject of the degree is of little or no consequence. Even for employers who value specialist knowledge it is still relatively unimportant because it has a short shelf-life (Table 2.1). Rather than value specialist knowledge for its own sake, the QHE research indicates that most employers:

- consider that understanding of core principles, technical ability, potential, and willingness to learn and continually update knowledge are more important than a stock of knowledge;

- consider problem-solving to be a very important attribute but one with which they are only moderately satisfied because of graduates' limited or non-existent experience of 'real world' problem-solving and of the application of understanding to such settings.

Employers are only moderately satisfied with the technical ability of graduates (Table 2.2). Indeed, graduates are not seen as particularly good at applying knowledge or understanding to practical work situations because they are unable to improvise, lack commercial awareness and lack appreciation of the human or cultural context within which they are working. They are novices, not experts: they have potential but have not yet learned to perform.

Table 2.2 *Employer ratings of satisfaction with graduate attributes*

Attribute	Mean	Rank
Willingness to learn	82.98	1
Cooperation	76.89	2
Desire to achieve/motivation	76.41	3
Ability to use information technology	76.04	4
Commitment	74.40	5
Self-motivation	74.21	6
Dependability/reliability	73.19	7
Flexibility	73.19	7

Attribute	Mean	Rank
Drive/energy	72.78	9
Numeracy	70.83	10
Equipped for continuous education	70.69	11
Team work	70.17	12
Adaptability (intellectual)	69.56	13
Self-confidence	68.70	14
Interest in lifelong learning	68.64	15
Enquiry and research skills	68.28	16
Analytic ability	67.08	17
Adaptability (organizational)	67.07	18
Logical argument	66.26	19
Persistence/tenacity	65.73	20
Consideration for others	65.55	21
Rapid conceptualization of issues	65.37	22
Understanding of core principles	65.24	23
Loyalty	65.04	24
Can deal with large amounts of information	64.75	25
Maturity	64.52	26
Initiative	64.50	27
Self-management	64.29	28
Technical ability	64.23	29
Curiosity	63.71	30
Can cope with pressure/stress	63.71	30
Problem-solving ability	63.33	32
Communication skills (oral)	61.88	33
Leadership potential	61.13	34
General knowledge	60.98	35
Critical ability	60.25	36
Imagination	60.21	37
Can summarize key issues	60.11	38
Tolerance	59.31	39
Planning ability	58.82	40
Organizational skills	58.61	41
Innovation	58.40	42
Creativity	58.40	42
Independent judgement	58.33	44
Tact	57.98	45
Time management	57.56	46
Ability to relate to wider context	57.26	47
Communication skills (written)	56.67	48
Specialist factual knowledge	56.30	49
Deep understanding	54.10	50
Problem-setting ability	54.03	51
Knowledge of social/political issues	53.72	52

Attribute	Mean	Rank
Experience of the world of work	53.57	53
Relevant work experience	53.39	54
Leadership ability	53.15	55
Influencing skills	51.90	56
Decision-making skills	51.68	57
Commercial awareness	49.79	58
Knowledge of the organization	48.53	59
Negotiation skills	47.88	60
Prior knowledge of the job	47.03	61
Financial knowledge or understanding	45.16	62

Intellect and adaptability

Employers want graduates to be flexible, adaptable and receptive to change. Employers expect graduates to exhibit a range of intellectual abilities. They want graduates who are inquisitive, innovative, logical, analytic, critical, creative, able to think laterally and conceptualize issues rapidly. Overall, employers:

- are unimpressed with the innovativeness of graduates, in part due to the graduates' insensitivity to the implications of innovation;

- are satisfied that graduates are analytic, logical, able to conceptualize issues rapidly and deal with large amounts of information;

- think that graduates' critical ability is not quite so satisfactory. There was some expressed dissatisfaction with the lateral thinking and synthetic ability of graduates;

- are satisfied with the flexibility and intellectual adaptability of graduates.

Working in an organization

Working in a modern organization requires an ability to cope with pressure, manage stress, meet deadlines, prioritize work and, most of all, be dependable. Team work is identified as the single most important skill by employers.

Employers were also looking for commitment, self-motivation, drive and desire to achieve. In general, employers:

- are satisfied with the dependability and organizational adaptability of graduates but far less satisfied with their ability to cope with pressure, time management and organizational skills;

- are satisfied with the commitment, self-motivation, drive and desire to achieve of graduates, although this may be because employers' recruitment procedures are designed to capture such individuals;

- consider graduates to have a poor understanding of the culture of a modern organization and tend to be naïve about industrial relations issues, organizational politics, knowing how to deal with people of different seniorities, and recognizing other people's motivations;

- are satisfied with graduates' ability to work in teams and with their cooperativeness.

Interpersonal skills

Interpersonal skills is an area that is often regarded as very important by graduate recruiters, but one where there is a gap between expectations and performance. Employers often refer to the:

- arrogance of graduates, particularly in terms of a common lack of recognition of skills and abilities of non-graduates. There is a fine line drawn between arrogance and self-confidence and it is the latter, not the former, which recruiters look for during the selection process;

- graduates' lack of awareness of the impact they make and their failure to realize that they have to gain the respect of peers and subordinates. It has been said that graduates think they know it all and often lack tact and tolerance;

- graduates' inability to relate to non-graduate employees. Graduates sometimes see themselves as a breed apart but employers want graduates who can communicate with people who are not on the same intellectual level.

Communication

Employers place a great deal of importance on graduates' communication skills, both oral and written. Communication skills, including listening, are important to employers because it is necessary for graduates in industry to communicate ideas and concepts efficiently and effectively to colleagues and customers, and to hear what is being meant as well as what is being said. Employers were:

- dissatisfied with both oral and written communication skills;

- often critical of graduates' grasp of fundamentals of written communication, especially basic grammar, sentence structure and punctuation;

- concerned about graduates' range of writing abilities. Graduates may be good at producing essays, laboratory reports, academic projects and dissertations but they are relatively poor at producing other forms of written communication;

- disappointed by graduates' inability to write reports. It seems that graduates have learned to provide balanced arguments that explore every nuance of a debate but are not experienced in making a persuasive case. Reports are much more prescriptive than essays and graduates are not good at writing them;

- unimpressed by graduates' oral presentation ability. Graduates seem to have had little experience of making, or being assessed on, oral presentations.

There is little evidence that employers or academics are seriously committed to working towards the European Commission's language policy for higher education.

The importance employers gave to information technology usage was not particularly high, although they were very satisfied with graduates' computer literacy. Some employers, though, noted that graduates are often more comfortable communicating with computers than with people.

CORE SKILLS

The QHE research suggests that employers value a set of generic or core skills and attitudes, including:

- willingness to learn
- team work
- communication skills
- problem-solving
- analytic ability
- logical argument
- ability to summarize key issues.

They also value a range of personal attributes, including:

- commitment
- energy
- self-motivation
- self-management
- reliability
- cooperation
- flexibility and adaptability.

It could plausibly be argued that most of these skills lie at the heart of the academic process. Higher education has always claimed to foster these skills and they are implicit in the undergraduate experience. Others reply that this is an idealized notion of the undergraduate experience, one that is under increasing threat from the transition from an elite to a mass higher education system and from reductions in the unit of resource. If higher education is to respond to employers' calls and to sustain a long-held claim to promote a range of qualities through liberal (and scientific and professional) education, then it is now necessary to ensure that the implicit contribution of higher education is made explicit and codified within a clearly identified and integrated set of aims, objectives, teaching and learning processes, outcomes and assessment methods.

WHAT CAN INDEPENDENT STUDY OFFER?

Independent study provides a useful way of *developing* a range of these desirable attributes, as will be briefly outlined below. Furthermore, it is also a means of *demonstrating* a diverse set of abilities to a potential employer. Willingness to learn, along with many of the personal attributes such as commitment, energy, self-motivation and flexibility, are not easy for graduates from standard, taught courses to demonstrate to employers.

The creation of an independent study programme is a dynamic process split into three distinct stages: a study proposal, fulfilment of the proposal, and assessment. At the former Polytechnic of East London, this was generally carried out over the course of an academic year and progression to the next year depended not only on achievement in the previous year, but also on the proposal for the next year's study. But, in general terms, student planning and reflection are integral parts of the learner's creation of the independent study programme. Independent study, by its very nature, is a vehicle for demonstrating proficiency in those attributes valued by employers.

The key issue, though, is not the demonstration of the range of core attributes, as useful as that is in the employment market. It is the extent to which independent study empowers students through the enhancement of such attributes. Some of these are briefly discussed in the following sections.

Willingness to learn

The single most important attribute of graduates is their willingness to learn and to continue to learn (Harvey with Green, 1994). Independent study is indicative of a willingness to learn and more importantly provides an initiation into the world of lifelong learning. Students interviewed by Ainley (1994) clearly identified the value of the specific learning skills that had been developed through IS:

[If] I wanted to study guitar or something, I could apply those learning skills to doing it. Using my own method that you've developed yourself rather than having a method that you've had thrust upon you... (p.129)

Instead of a structured learning programme provided by a conventional taught course, independent study places the onus on the student to identify a programme of self-learning.

Team work and cooperation

Team working and cooperative activity would appear to be the Achilles' heel of independent learning. This assumes that independent learning is solitary learning. However, much independent learning is also linked into cooperative endeavours and reference-team building. At Lancaster University, for example, the first year of IS has, for most students, almost entirely focused upon cooperative team working activity.

Even where there is less emphasis on the development of teams, independent study does not involve a student disappearing to work alone in dusty archives or undertaking fieldwork in an isolated setting. On the contrary, independent study often involves collaborating in a variety of settings with external organizations, or at the very least working closely with a tutor. Indeed, grave concern is expressed if students disappear and make no attempt to relate to the support structures set up for independent study.

Communication skills

Independent study programmes require a great deal of communication, often with different audiences. As this demands a variety of communication modes, IS students have the opportunity to develop a range of communicative competences that may be more extensive than is the case with the majority of students on traditional courses. For example, the communication skills demonstrated through a presentation by a student on a standard single-subject degree programme are often limited by the audience of peers and tutor from the same subject area. The audience is familiar with the concepts and language used in the presentation. The IS student in a similar situation presenting work before an IS peer group, or a wider group including people from outside the university, cannot rely on this familiarity, which makes considerably greater demands on the deployment of a selection from the range of communicative competences.

In addition, from the start of the independent study programme, students must become adept at negotiation skills in order to have their study plans and learning contracts accepted. This need for negotiation skills will continue with tutor liaison, and extends often through external, collaborative ventures within the community or with local employers.

Problem-solving

Problem-solving lies at the heart of most independent study projects. The knowledge sought by students in the fulfilment of their study plan provides the backdrop for the acquisition of many skills but at the centre is the art of problem-solving. Indeed, a student interviewed by Ainley (1994) saw independent study going beyond problem-solving:

> Now I see Independent Study as having some kind of quality whereby people can be more creative in their approaches to their work and in that express their own meaning a bit more accurately, a bit more freely – freely is probably a better word. It's a different approach to... what shall we say?... problem-solving. It's more to do with developing the intellectual potential of the human brain. (p.127)

Unlike the student on the standard study programme, IS students have to identify their own core textbooks. In essence, in locating the solutions to the objectives that they have set out for themselves, they have to identify both the keys and the doors. The instruction that independent study gives to its students consists principally of how to *gain* knowledge rather than the knowledge itself.

> Perhaps most importantly, I find that because IS doesn't teach you so much a specific knowledge, it teaches you how to gain knowledge, that's what it teaches you and that's the most important thing in journalism, how to gain knowledge on your own account, off your own back and I've learnt that, that's for sure. (Ainley, 1994, p.133)

Analytic ability, logical argument, and ability to summarize key issues

Independent study provides no more opportunities for these activities than does a conventional course of study. The nature of work, what is assessed and the kind of assessment processes will be major determinants of students' grasp of these qualities. Yet, within independent study it is left to the student to design the assessment method as well as the programme of study and so it might be argued that this design further stimulates and challenges the IS students to develop and demonstrate these skills at each stage of the proposed programme of study.

Self-motivation, self-management and commitment

Undergraduate independent study is similar to postgraduate study in encouraging a rigorous self-discipline. Despite tutorial support and reference peer groups, independent study requires considerable self-motivation and self-management along with a clear commitment to complete a programme of work within a given time frame (see also Chapter 3). There is the individual responsibility for managing and fulfilling the learning contract that binds the students to their agreed study proposal. These skills are vital to the success of any independent study programme and it follows that if employers understood the nature of these programmes, they could well see them as ideal exemplifications of these skills.

Flexibility and adaptability

What employers want more than anything are continuing learners who are adaptable and flexible. The experience of independent study, which invariably requires considerable flexibility and adaptability to deal with unforeseen circumstances and to strive towards a result, is an ideal training for such attributes. The annual assessment of the students' study plans often requires that they should not only be willing to adapt and change, but more importantly that they should be able to anticipate the need to adapt and change.

CONCLUSION

While it is clear from the QHE research that employers can identify specific graduate attributes that are desirable, it may be suggested that the sum total of what employers desire could be encapsulated in the term 'the reflective practitioner'. If not a fully developed reflective practitioner, employers desire a graduate who has the ability soon to become a reflective practitioner within the chosen profession. Professional organizations are clearly moving the structure and content of professional education towards the reflective practitioner model (Harvey and Mason, 1995). It is here that independent study makes its greatest contribution towards producing the quality graduate desired by employers. Reflection is an integral part of the independent study process: it is necessary in the development of the programme and recognized as an important skill gained by Ainley's students:

> I've learnt and I will remember much more than I would have done on a conventional course... I did a dissertation and it's all based on coursework and then you write a review saying how you learnt things and what you'd do differently; you evaluate your own work. (Ainley, 1994, p.130)

The potential to transform an organization was another quality employers identified as being particularly important in their choice of graduate employees. Transformation should play a part in any quality higher education programme, but whereas transformation within conventional degrees is shaped by the tutor, lecturer or course designer, within independent study the impetus for transformation comes principally from the students.

The combination of reflection, transformation and the acquisition of the high-level skills of critique, analysis and interpretation, forms the basis of the reflective practitioner. Independent study hones these skills and abilities, utilizing the subject-specific knowledge identified within the students' own study plans as a backdrop for development. This does not make the subject-specific knowledge unimportant: indeed it is often responsible for maintaining students' interest throughout a long and demanding course.

The ethos of independent study may not orient it towards the production of graduate employment-fodder. However, independent study does have the power to create highly employable people precisely because its focus is the development of the individual. The changes within the destabilized employment sector reflect the need for highly motivated individuals, capable of being responsible for and managing their own career progression (Bailey, 1990). In this context, the attributes developed in an independent study programme can be seen as a reflection of the attributes desired by employers.

Chapter 3

Independent study, independent studies and 'core skills' in higher education

Peter Knight

INTRODUCTION

Nationally, there is no shortage of enthusiasm for curriculum developments that encourage learners to be more self-directed, more capable and more enterprising. In many ways the problem is that these goals are characterized by competing projects such as Enterprise in Higher Education, Learner-managed Learning, Education for Capability, self-directed learning, flexible learning, experiential learning, open learning, resource-based learning, independent study and self-regulated learning. They are seen as members of a family of concepts, a family that is widely valued because its members allow learners to develop and demonstrate desirable skills. These skills are seen to be worthwhile and appropriate to higher education (Brookfield, 1985; Dart and Clarke, 1991; Dressel and Thompson, 1973; Fowler, 1993; Percy and Ramsden, 1980; Stephenson, 1993; Zimmerman, 1990).

Yet there is a danger that the enthusiasm for this family concept may be a mixed blessing. I shall present data from one study of a department of Independent Studies (IS). It will be shown that it is a complex matter for this department to develop learner autonomy and that the department might be well advised to put its programmes on a more structured footing. Against this, attempts to promote independent learning by allowing students to take one or two dissertation or project modules look inadequate. This, though, is a significant way in which independent learning is being made available to learners in higher education. It is a poor shadow of what an IS programme might offer, let alone what might be done were changes made on the lines recommended. If this is the future of IS, it is about to become both more common and more superficial: to be marginalized through tokenism.

THREATS TO IS PROGRAMMES

Independent study needs to be independent study of something and much of the writing on independent learning (eg, Graves, 1993) assumes that it will take place within a mainstream degree course, representing an opportunity for students to apply disciplinary insights themselves. This fits with those views of learning that hold that effective learning depends upon general learning ability of the sort that independent study might promote and upon understanding and knowledge of the discipline within which learning is taking place. This is not a negligible point. Discussing the aims of higher education, Atkins (1995) has insisted that the pursuit of personal transferable skills may be misguided (because psychological research has cast doubts upon their transferability) and that it is not distinctive of higher education (because even infants have curricula intended to foster these skills). Her suggestion is that such skills should be taught and will mainly be applied within the context of a distinctive body of knowledge that is to be understood in terms of its content and of its distinctive ways of working and tests of truth. On this view, being a good scientist does depend upon a robust, general competence but it also depends upon knowing a lot about scientific methods, processes and phenomena. Competence is not, then, divorced from knowledge. This view may have uncomfortable implications for IS programmes in which there is no requirement that student learning centres upon a coherent body of knowledge.

A second threat to IS programmes is that there continues to be a national trend towards allowing students to negotiate the shape of module assessment and the range of assessment techniques that are routinely deployed has been extended. It is becoming increasingly appreciated that independent learning is something that is desirable in its own right. HEFCE guidelines on the assessment of teaching quality say that assessors 'will wish to see students encouraged to take responsibility for much of their own learning'. Many academic departments now incorporate some independent learning into modules (sometimes as a way of reducing tutors' contact time), and a significant number allow – or require – students to do dissertations and projects. The rise of independent learning can be seen as the biggest threat to IS: after all, why learn independently in IS when mainstream subject departments seem to offer the same thing in familiar surroundings?

It has been suggested that IS programmes may be under threat at a time when the concept of independent learning is becoming more attractive. I shall now present data drawn from an evaluation of a department offering a complete degree programme in IS. In discussing these data I shall identify a number of key issues in independent *learning*, and argue that independent learning should not be entrusted to serendipity: it needs to be seen in terms of the development and application of a set of core skills. Acknowledging the associated problems of definition, pedagogy and assessment, I shall argue that it is hard to advance these even through a complete programme of IS, hence unrealistic to make great claims about what can be achieved where students experience a smattering of modules that are based on independent learning.

VIEWS OF STUDENTS AND PROSPECTIVE STUDENTS

Responses from SEDA members

Staff and Educational Development Association (SEDA) members were sent a one-page questionnaire in which they were asked to answer three questions relating to the idea of independent learning and IS. The response rate of 32 per cent was greater than this postal survey was expected to yield. It was possible to explore some of the responses further at the SEDA conference in late May 1994.

The first question invited SEDA colleagues to identify things that learners need to master if they are to become more autonomous. Data were analysed by listing every separate suggestion made by respondents and then grouping them through iterative content analysis.

Nearly three-quarters of the ideas could be grouped under four headings. Twenty-nine per cent of the responses held that to become independent learners, people need to become competent in planning and time management. Awareness of the learning process and of one's own skills as a learner came second (24 per cent of responses). In addition, some general, transferable skills are needed, such as communication skills and skills with IT (12 per cent of responses) as are more domain-specific research skills (11 per cent). It goes without saying that it cannot be presumed that students enter higher education with these skills in place. They have to be learned, which may mean that they have to be taught.

This was the focus of the second question to SEDA members. There was a greater range of answers and the three largest sets of responses only account for 54 per cent of the total. There was a strong opinion, accounting for almost one-third of the points made, that a structure has to be provided within which learner autonomy can be developed: it cannot be left to chance. The second category (13 per cent of responses) comprised suggestions that negotiation, through learning contracts and records of achievement (RoAs), for example, is a powerful way of advancing learner autonomy. Third, there was a notable body of opinion (11 per cent) that such autonomy should be promoted through subject departments who would also be responsible for providing the enabling structure commended in the first category.

Finally, colleagues were asked how the appeal of the IS programme to undergraduates might be strengthened. Again, the main response was that it would be helpful to make it clear to students that autonomy was to be developed within a structure (25 per cent of responses to this question). It was thought that learning contracts and RoAs would be attractive (12 per cent). Workplace learning was also identified as a powerful way of promoting the appeal of IS (10 per cent) and it was also thought that group learning or action learning sets would be a selling point (8 per cent). A large number of eclectic points defied any attempt at meaningful classification.

It is clear that these experts agreed that becoming an independent learner involves gaining competence in some areas and that it is a university's responsibility to ensure that there is an enabling structure in place to support that process.

Survey of students not taking IS modules

Fifty students chosen at random at one university were interviewed to clarify their understanding of the work of a department of IS.

The major benefit to students of doing IS courses was said to be that choice was available so that interests could be followed and a degree programme could be broadened (49 per cent of responses to this question). Some responses (6 per cent) mentioned that research and enquiry skills could be learnt, others (7 per cent) alluded to the benefits of autonomous learning and a further 11 per cent pointed to the way that confidence and self-discipline would be enhanced through IS work. Seven per cent of responses suggested that the programme would be enjoyable, while a few (4 per cent) thought that it would be helpful in the quest for employment.

The second question asked them what they believed to be the disadvantages of an IS programme. A large set of disadvantages was identified, all centring on perceptions of the experience of working independently. Fears of isolation were identified and associated with the perceived lack of structure and problems in working with directors of studies (these are tutors in subject departments who supervise a unit of independent study on a topic in which they have expertise). It was thought that this would make considerable demands on self-discipline and motivation and a further 7 per cent of responses were that IS is a demanding programme. There were also fears (22 per cent of responses) that IS lacked prestige and that there might be difficulties in getting employers to recognize it.

It appears that while valuing the choice, or absence of constraint, that goes with IS, students who did not take IS modules feared that they might not be sufficiently supported and that they could be rather isolated as a result.

Survey of IS Part 2 students

All students registered for Part 2 IS modules, taken in the second and third years, were sent a questionnaire that had been constructed on the basis of a review of departmental papers and then piloted. The four major perceived strengths of the IS programme were that, 'You can choose your topics for study' (17 per cent); 'You can work at your own pace' (12 per cent); 'It's enjoyable' (11 per cent); and that 'You get marketable skills' (11 per cent).

They were also invited to complete a closed-response questionnaire addressing the perceived weaknesses of the programme. The five most common responses were that 'People don't recognize how demanding it is' (17 per cent); 'It's very time-consuming' (14 per cent); 'People don't recognize how valuable it is' (10 per cent); 'The quality of supervision is variable' (10 per cent); and that 'other subject staff are disdainful of IS' (10 per cent).

Two themes seem to pervade these students' views. One is that IS is deceptive – it demands a lot more than outsiders realize. The other is that these students value the choice that IS gives them.

Survey of students in FE colleges

Focus groups were run in four FE colleges. Participants were given a brochure entry for IS which had been edited to remove all references to IS. The programme that was described was simply identified as one run by a university department. Discussion focused on participants' reactions to this text in the light of their own situations and ambitions. No significant misunderstandings of the text were detected in the course of these discussions.

The most popular feature of the brochure text was 'freedom to construct your own degree scheme' (20 mentions), closely followed by the concept of relative freedom from traditional exams (17). The practical project work was chosen as a positive feature by 11 students. Sixteen students from this group picked the availability of tutorial support and guidance as a major selling point and nine particularly liked the idea of working in small student support groups. As might be anticipated with a group containing a majority of mature students with domestic commitments, many (13) liked the flexibility to arrange study around other commitments.

The anxieties raised by the brochure text were more varied. Some of the fears were that IS:

- was non-conventional (4)
- lacked structure (3)
- would lead to problems with directors of study and with academic supervision (4)
- required a lot of self-discipline (2).

One student used the following phrases: 'Jack of all trades and master of none. If you yourself don't know, how do you know your needs? How will this equip you for living when you leave university? Employers may not need it.' These concerns echo those expressed by students on-course in the university.

Survey of 17-year-old university aspirants

Questionnaires were used to cover the same ground with these respondents as was covered with the FE students through the focus groups. Some 500 were completed. They favoured the programme because it offers them less traditional methods of assessment (37 per cent of all factors mentioned). Flexibility (27 per cent) and the individualized programme (22 per cent) were also prominent selling points.

In terms of assessment methods, 17-year-olds were particularly keen to avoid examinations: 'Less traditional methods mean I don't have to do an exam and I can work at my own pace instead of cramming at the end of the year'.

Other students found the idea of alternative assessment exciting: 'Multimedia is a great idea because I can concentrate on what I am good at'.

Flexibility was a another favourite. Students like the idea of being able to fit into their degrees their 'other commitments'. The idea of 'making-up a course as you go along' attracted many of the students located in this category.

Individuality scored highly, primarily for its perceived role in allowing a degree course to be constructed 'according to individual needs'. Students were not more specific as to what these individual needs were but several mentioned the benefits of constructing a course which takes into account 'my strengths and weaknesses'.

Negative reasons were concentrated in the categories of 'lack of clear assessment' (22 per cent – clearly a polarizing category), 'employer suspicion' (21 per cent) and 'lack of tutoring' (17 per cent).

Potential students appear to value the choice that the IS programme gives, but to be concerned that there might be insufficient structure and uneasy about the marketplace value of an IS degree.

Summary of the empirical studies

This evidence shows that there is a widespread belief that an IS programme should not be a matter of serendipity but should embody a structured progression towards independence. Difficulties and fears have been noticed. Eight points may be highlighted:

- However independent the students' learning is, it should not be inchoate: some structure is wanted. SEDA members suggested some of the elements that might be included in such a structure. These elements would need development to indicate different levels of mastery of these competences, which would then become a set of core learning goals. However, the opportunity should be retained for learners to develop their own, alternative structures.

- The fears and worries suggest that independent learning was seen as something quite demanding and even threatening.

- There was also a consistent feeling that the value of this approach was unrecognized.

- Choice and flexibility were highly valued. We could characterize these as negative features of learner autonomy – independent learning is not valued because it promotes certain competences but because the learner is not constrained by the usual structures of higher education.

- Non-traditional assessment methods were valued especially by learners and aspirant students, although they were also a source of concern to 17-year-olds.

- Working with peers is valued and might be emphasized as one response to fears that independent learning could be isolated learning.

- IS helps the development of better self- and time management.

- IS may help the development of metacognition.

IMPLICATIONS FOR INDEPENDENT *LEARNING*

The advantages that have been associated with the IS programme are the sort of things that many wish to see HE develop. Of course, these advantages are associated with a particularly open curriculum and a very individualist view of independent study. It is likely that a different approach to IS, or to independent learning, would lead to a somewhat different list of benefits.

It has also been shown that students feel that they need to learn how to be independent learners, calling for both structure and support. Hampson (1994) has shown how students doing dissertations, a form of independent study, have the same fears. On two grounds, then, it is possible to reject a 'serendipity' approach to becoming an independent learner, an approach in which students are expected to discover how to become independent through being left to work on their own. One ground is that in this way there is no guarantee that a particular set of goals will be achieved. The other is that students (and SEDA members) want guidance in the form of some type of structure. While this is perfectly consistent with the work of Vygotsky, who argued that through working with others we come to be able to do things alone that were previously beyond us, it seems to sit uneasily with the notion of *independent* learning. A Vygotskian approach implies a structure and the use of 'scaffolding' to help us progress up that structure. Independent learning implies going it alone, unaided. Yet, the implication is misleading. Independence is a goal, not a starting point. There is a sense in which we have to learn, and perhaps to be 'taught' to be independent. Independence comes from mastery. And mastery may need to be purposefully promoted through an enabling structure.

This raises sharply the issue of what might comprise such a structure. Clearly, it will not be a content-led structure and, although it is possible to see that independent learning within a subject area might depend upon a mastery of core concepts, this is less compelling than saying that the structure of independent learning, and its goals, might best be seen in terms of core skills. Mastering these key ways of working is a route to independence and an encouragement to a desirable, 'deep' approach to learning. Independence, then, is not the absence of guidance but the outcome of a process of learning that enables learners to work with such guidance as they wish to take, whether it be from peers, from electronic media, or from tutors.

These key ways of working might be referred to as 'core skills' but their nature is contentious. A little-noticed problem is that 'skills' are a construct to help us to think about human capability. It is not evident that thinking in terms of skills (or of competences) is the best way to think about human capability, and there is considerable argument about what these skills might be (Knight, 1985). It is important to identify any such skills that would be fitting for and distinctive of a programme of *higher* education. Also, these skills are not necessarily transferable. There is a substantial literature on the transfer of training and it tends to say that transfer is not easy nor reliable. Consequently, the assessment of such skills is problematic since the solution to any task depends upon our interpretation of its context and content, as well as upon our mastery of the relevant skills, information and concepts. Finally, we have little beyond common sense to help us to identify appropriate pedagogies for developing such skills. Since substantial discussion would be needed before answers to these questions could be proposed, the approach taken here is to show something of the possibilities.

- Core skills might be chosen from research into the qualities that employers look for in university graduates (eg, Harvey with Green, 1994). Some of these qualities are 'personal qualities' and there are reservations about both the desirability and the practicality of trying to foster these through higher education programmes.

- GNVQ core skills – using IT, communication and the application of number – might serve as a structure. However, they have not been developed for higher education, and it may be that new skills, such as argumentation, need to be developed.[1]

- Enquiry skills, sometimes known as research methods, might be purposefully developed.

- Cognitive skills, perhaps based upon Bloom's problematic *Taxonomy*, might become the goals of independent learning in higher education.

- Metacognition means thinking about our thinking. There is some evidence that metacognitive learners are better learners, more aware of their learning strategies and more adept at applying strategies that are fit for the purposes in hand. In professional courses, the (overworked) notion of the reflective practitioner can be seen as an expression of metacognition. A fuller discussion of this point and of core skills in general is in Harvey and Knight (1996, ch.7).

From this brief review, four conclusions may be advanced concerning the development of independent learning in HE:

1. 'Independence' is a contentious concept. Without an understanding of what we mean by the term, the development of independent learning will be haphazard at best.

2. There may be good reasons – such as saving tutor time, or facilitating distance learning – for putting some modules on an independent study basis. It cannot be assumed that learners will be well-equipped to cope with them. Nor, unless these articulate a developed vision of independence in learning, can strong claims be made about their contribution to learner autonomy.

3. If we wish learners to become skilled at working independently, a structure needs to be provided to help them. This also implies that tutors have embraced a view of what it takes and of what it means to be an independent learner. It is hard to see how such a structure will be devised without grappling with the vexed notion of core skills (or competences).

4. The serendipity approach to independent learning will suit some learners and it is attractive for hard-pressed tutors seeking to reduce their contact hours. However, where there is a programme goal of helping all learners to become more independent, then this will not do. Indeed, such a goal probably means that tutors will have to work more, not less. In particular, they will have to think very hard about goals, structures and support. Questions of assessment and pedagogy are not negligible.

The view has been developed that independent learning and IS ought not to be defined negatively, that is by saying that they represent an absence of tutor action. This may be the desired end-state, but getting there needs considerable insightful planning and action.

ACKNOWLEDGEMENTS

This chapter has benefited from conversations with John Wakeford and Jo Tait at Lancaster and with Dave O'Reilly at the University of East London. David Boud's comments at the 1994 seminar led me to clarify some of the points made here. If things remain unclear, odd or defective, it is my fault.

NOTE

1. I owe this point to Dr C Boys of the National Council for Vocational Qualifications.

Chapter 4

Do students value a flexible educational experience?

Hazel Knox

INTRODUCTION

Credit Accumulation and Transfer schemes (CATs) provide an effective vehicle for responding to changing conditions both within higher education and beyond it in the employment marketplace. They offer flexibility and student choice and 'extend learning opportunities in higher education to the largest number of eligible students' (Robertson, 1994). The CATs introduced at the University of Paisley certainly meets these criteria. The scheme was launched in September 1990 with 32 part-time students enrolled on a combined studies degree programme and four years later had over 2,000 students enrolled on a variety of credit accumulation and transfer degrees. In the main these students would not have entered higher education were it not for the flexible opportunities offered by CATs.

However, not only are the numbers of participants in CATs at the University of Paisley and elsewhere showing a year-on-year increase, but the students so recruited are increasingly diverse in nature. Institutions must respond to the administrative and academic challenges of ensuring that the CATs student experience, which will be different from that of the traditional student, is equally valid and of equal quality. Similarly, students must respond to the opportunities afforded by credit accumulation and transfer by assuming responsibility as active participants in their own learning processes.

THE NEED FOR INSTITUTIONAL CHANGE

Much of the attractiveness of CATs lies in the flexibility such schemes permit. The scheme at Paisley enables flexibility in terms of:

- mode of attendance: which may include full- or part-time study, day or evening classes and permits study to continue throughout the calendar and not just the academic year;

38

- mode of delivery: which may include attending lectures, laboratories and seminars, pursuing independent study projects and/or engaging in work-based learning;

- point of entry: which is determined by the amount of learning the individual has already undertaken; both accredited prior learning (APL) and accredited prior experiential learning (APEL) may be imported, if appropriate;

- choice of subjects: which allows individual programmes of study to be negotiated, choosing from the full range of university provision;

- choice of exit award: which ranges from Certificate of Higher Education to honours degree for undergraduates and from Certificate to Masters at postgraduate level;

- choice of award title: which reflects the major subject area(s) studied.

Introducing such flexibility has significant consequences for both the institution and the student, and demands a rapid response to the need for changes in policy, in practice and, importantly, in attitudes towards higher education itself. The concept of a course is no longer tenable in the context of CATs since programmes of study vary from student to student in content, in duration and in mode of attendance and delivery. All programmes are individually tailored and many will remain unique. By tailoring the programme to meet the needs and aspirations of the individual, it becomes personalized, relevant, and owned. Hence the student is put into an active rather than a passive role and from the outset becomes an important participant in the design of his or her programme of study.

This flexibility is in stark contrast to the traditional provision at Paisley, where a strong reputation has been built up for providing high quality, vocationally relevant higher education. However, as MacLennan (1995) argued, being vocationally relevant has generally meant that courses have been designed with specific occupations and the recognition of particular professional institutions in mind. Such courses are largely predefined in character and offer little choice to the student. This structure may be appropriate in some subject areas but, in general, higher education institutions must constantly be aware that in many other areas 'yesterday's courses are unlikely to be the most appropriate for tomorrow's world' (Ball, 1989).

Needless to say, the arrival of CATs within such a traditional, course-based institution sent 'shock waves reverberating through its academic community' (MacLennan, 1995). However, the interesting and rather unusual characteristic of the introduction of CATs at Paisley is that it did take place within this persistently traditional framework. The centralized academic and administrative changes which normally precede CATs within an institution (for example modular provision within a semester framework) did not happen at Paisley. Instead, a small CATs unit, later renamed the Centre for CATs and Continuing Education, nourished by funding from both the university and BP Exploration, adopted an independent approach which in practice necessitated duplicating many of the activities associated with running a full-scale higher education institution. These activities include providing student guidance, marketing, processing applications and handling admissions, participating in academic programme design, validating individual programmes of study, accrediting courses, and ensuring students are accurately tracked throughout their university career. For the latter a customized management information system, the CATs database, was developed. In essence, the Centre for CATs and Continuing Education 'operates as a University within a University' (Knox and MacLennan, 1994).

With the advent of CATs, institutional change and an extensive programme of staff development were essential, as was bringing about a revolution in staff and student attitudes towards the educational experience. Students have to accept responsibility for their learning, which may extend from the stage of presenting their prior learning portfolio, through negotiation of year-by-year programmes of study, to the selection of those subjects which generate their preferred exit award and title. The importance of guidance, which is obviously at the heart of the process of making appropriate and informed choices, has always been acknowledged, and a sizeable team of education guidance advisers has been established within the CATs office.

The empowerment of students to determine and direct their own learning means that many elements of traditional academic authority are devolved from the committees whose members design and run courses, to the individual students who devise programmes of study. Acceptance of this situation is difficult for many academic staff who interpret it as a threat to their authority. However, much can be done to offset such perceptions by positive internal marketing, the organization of staff development seminars and the widespread dissemination of information on student progress and performance. The students themselves are often the best ambassadors, both within the institution and outside. They tend to be highly motivated and from their work and personal backgrounds contribute valuable practical experiences to lecture and seminar situations.

In addition to bringing about change in the administrative structures of the university, winning over the hearts and minds of the academic community and engaging students actively in their own learning, many very practical considerations require attention when flexible study opportunities are introduced. Part-time students make particular demands on the facilities of the university. Whether they attend on a day or evening basis, it cannot be assumed that opening hours designed to meet the needs of full-timers will also meet their needs. Many changes have been introduced at Paisley to accommodate the needs of this significant group of students; for example, the library now opens on Sundays, janitorial and security services are maintained until 10 pm, nursery facilities are available for students with young children, and the CATs office has an education guidance adviser on duty from 9 am until at least 7 pm daily during term time.

CATS AT THE UNIVERSITY OF PAISLEY

There is no doubt that CATs at the University of Paisley has been hugely successful. Figure 4.1 shows the growth in the number of enrolled students during the first five years of operation of the scheme.

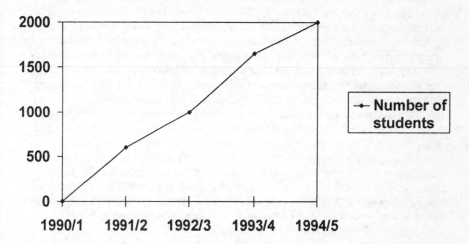

Figure 4.1 *Increase in numbers of students enrolled over first five years*

The impact of CATs on overall university student numbers has been significant. CATs students accounted for approximately 30 per cent of the new entrants to the university in 1994/95 and now make up almost 25 per cent of the total student population. For the university, the CATs scheme is making a vital contribution to the maintenance of a viable student population in a period of relatively flat growth in the number of traditional entrants. However, the claim that the Paisley CATs is hugely successful is not based solely on student numbers: it is also amply verified in the evidence of widening access, satisfactory student performance and the provision of a valued experience.

Widening access to higher education can be confirmed by reference to a number of different criteria, for example the number of part-time students, the age distribution, the proportion of female students and the extent of credit transfer taking place. Historically, the University of Paisley, like many other higher education institutions, has recruited few part-time students, mainly school-leavers and under-21s, more males than females, and a minority with recognized prior credit. In the past, such factors have often militated against adults wishing to enter or return to higher education.

Facilitating part-time study has been a major feature of CATs at Paisley. For very many students, the flexibility of part-time routes into and through higher education provides the only feasible opportunity for them to participate. All 32 students in the initial CATs scheme intake in 1990/91 were part-timers, and although today a considerable number of full-time students enrol, the majority of students are following part-time study routes. Of the 1,618 students enrolled in 1993/94 only 33 per cent were full-timers. Of the 1,090 part-time students, just over 10 per cent attended during the day and the remainder were part-time evening students. The university has acknowledged that 'to make part-time study truly feasible for many people, it is important to keep the campus open for evening classes' (Caul, 1993). The vast majority of part-time students continue working while studying, mostly in full-time employment. Students can thus combine working with study and access higher education without having to give up the other commitments and demands in their lives. As one part-time student said, 'I can earn and learn!' Financial pressures, of course, also affect full-time students – approximately 40 per cent of the 1993/94 full-time CATs students were also combining part-time work with study. As reported by one evening student: 'I can't afford to give up work, so the flexibility of CATs in allowing part-time study is ideal for me'.

As shown in Figure 4.2, the age distribution of the 1993/94 CATs student population further testifies to the widening access afforded by the scheme. The mean student age was 30.4 years: 31.7 years for females, 28.5 years for males. Corresponding figures for 1992/93 were 32.2, 33.2 and 30.8 years respectively. Within this population it cannot be claimed that the majority of students are school-leavers or under 21!

A high proportion of female students has been a consistent feature of the CATs intakes. In 1991/92, 1992/93 and 1993/94 the proportions of female students have been 61 per cent, 60 per cent and 61 per cent respectively, further evidence of the success of CATs in widening access to a group traditionally under-represented in higher education.

The majority of students take advantage of the facility to transfer credit into their current programme of study, importing APL, APEL or both. Of the 770 students entering CATs for the first time in 1993/94 only 75 (just under 10 per cent) entered without prior credit. Approximately 28 per cent entered with prior credit from professional qualifications, 46 per cent with credit from other further or higher education institutions and the remaining 17 per cent transferred with credit from another degree course within the university itself. In a recent survey of students and graduates, over 60 per cent considered 'credit given for prior certificates and experiential learning' as one of the most attractive of the flexible features of CATs.

As CATs students may be full- or part-time, may enter and exit at various stages, and may opt to take time out as other demands on their lives require, the question arises of how to define success in a credit accumulation and transfer scheme. The traditional measure of cohort progression rate, based on the proportion of students on a course progressing to the next stage of that course, is obviously no longer tenable. In CATs terms the accumulation of credit is not a prerequisite for continuing in the scheme and the assumption that all students are studying the same subjects and for the same overall amount of credit cannot be made.

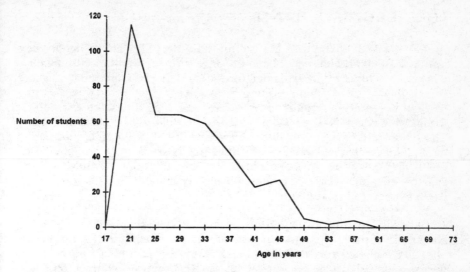

Figure 4.2 *The age distribution of the 1993/94 CATS student population*

One very crude way to measure success is in terms of the overall number of credit points gained as a percentage of the overall number of credit points attempted by the various sub-groups within the overall student population. Using this measure, the results for 1990–93 show that the overall success rate rose steadily during this period, from 65 per cent in 1990/91 to 83 per cent in 1992/93. Much of this rise can be attributed to improved guidance and admissions procedures, particularly for part-time (evening) students.

Such success rates are very gratifying, bearing in mind that the profile of CATs students is quite unlike a traditional university population. In many ways the heterogeneity of CATs students make them a very vulnerable population, given the other financial, employment, social and domestic demands and responsibilities in their lives. The overall performance of part-time evening students is particularly encouraging. The success rate of this group in 1992/93 was 86 per cent, compared with 81 per cent for part-time (day) students and 64 per cent for full-time students.

Among those who complete their studies, high motivation to succeed is apparent. However, withdrawal rates throughout the academic session are high among part-timers, which to some extent may explain the differential between the success rates of full- and part-time students. The main reasons for withdrawal among part-time students are work-related, for example relocation to another work site or changed shift patterns which were incompatible with continuing part-time study. It is satisfying to have evidence that students who take advantage of the flexibility of CATs cope so well with the academic demands of their programmes of study.

THE STUDENT EXPERIENCE

In 1989 Kenneth Baker, then Minister of Education, said 'knowledge for its own sake is not and has never been the only value of importance in higher education'. This is a view expanded by Caul (1993) who argues that universities must do more than merely impart knowledge; they also have a duty to facilitate the intellectual and personal development of their students, that is to contribute actively to the value-added components of higher education. There are, of course, major difficulties to be faced in the definition and measurement of value-added, difficulties which are sharply brought into focus when assessing the value-added for diverse groups of students, for example school-leavers compared with mature students or full-time compared with part-time students.

As part of the University of Paisley's quality assurance procedure, all enrolled students receive an annual evaluation questionnaire which they may return if they wish, and which is returned anonymously. In this questionnaire, comments are invited on overall workload, individual subjects and tutors, volume and type of assessments, aspects of university provision and perceptions of the student experience. In 1993/94 CATs students were asked additional questions in which value-added was defined largely by the respondents themselves. Respondents were asked to rate the importance of the following as attributes of an effective employee and the extent to which they felt the CATs student experience provided opportunities for acquiring these qualities:

- oral communication skills

- written communication skills

- social skills

- transferable skills

- cognitive skills (analysis, synthesis and evaluation)

- specialist knowledge

- independence

- being an autonomous learner.

Almost all students (99 per cent) rated 'oral communication skills' as a very important factor in ensuring an effective employee; 98 per cent also perceived 'written communication skills' as very important. 'Independence' and 'being an autonomous learner' were rated as relatively unimportant by 42 per cent and 36 per cent of respondents respectively. Interestingly, fewer than half considered 'specialist knowledge' as important (see also Chapter 2). No one believed 'age' to be related to one's effectiveness as an employee.

The CATs student experience was perceived as providing the opportunity to acquire 'specialist knowledge', 'cognitive skills', 'transferable skills' and 'written communication skills' by 84 per cent, 73 per cent, 71 per cent and 65 per cent of respondents respectively. However, opportunities for acquiring 'oral communication skills' and 'social skills' were recognized by only approximately half of the students (54 per cent and 47 per cent).

Approximately 80 per cent considered 'specialist knowledge' important and agreed that the CATs student experience did provide opportunities for its acquisition; whereas the view that important 'oral communication skills' and 'social skills' were not acquired was expressed by approximately half of all respondents in each group. However, this is not necessarily a cause for great concern. As indicated earlier, the majority of CATs students at Paisley are mature students attending university on a part-time basis and they may already be socially skilled and able to communicate clearly, hence they do not look to their experience as a student to contribute *per se* to their personal development in these areas, as illustrated in the following comment made by one recent graduate: 'My job in marketing demands good interpersonal skills. I have not needed to acquire such skills from my experience as a student at university'.

A comparative study of the responses of students and graduates showed that there was general agreement between responses of the two groups (Spearman's rank order correlation coefficients of +0.95 and +0.96 on the factors related to employee effectiveness and on opportunities to acquire them through the CATs scheme respectively). The graduates were slightly more positive than students about the opportunities to acquire valued skills. This may be as a result of mature reflection on the student experience with the benefit of hindsight, or may be a consequence of being in work and finding out by experience what attributes are indeed of greatest value in a work setting. Overall there was an encouraging, positive message in the findings.

Many of the qualitative comments given by students in response to a number of open-ended questions about the benefits of accessing higher education flexibly also reflected very positive reactions to the opportunities presented by the scheme, for example 'I gained a real sense of worth, self-esteem and achievement' and, 'I gained valuable life experience'.

CONCLUSION

After its first five years of operation, the achievements of CATs at the University of Paisley are demonstrated by the quantitative data of participating numbers and success rates together with the qualitative data of positive student evaluation and comment.

The evidence confirms that students do wish to take advantage of the flexible opportunities afforded by credit accumulation and transfer. CATs extends access to significant groups of individuals who have traditionally been under-represented in higher education, in particular mature adults who are in secure employment with professional or other qualifications.

Being able to attend part-time enables them to study at their own pace, and the facility to switch between study modes can serve to minimize pressure on financial and other personal resources. Learners can increase or decrease the amount of study undertaken in line with career demands on time and with their own need for knowledge. Empowering students to take an active role in the negotiation of their individualized programmes of study means they take ownership of them and ensures that the future learning they undertake should be relevant and meet personal and professional needs. Undoubtedly, the flexibility of CATs is attractive and contributes to a valued student experience.

Chapter 5

The unexpected outcomes of critical professional learning

Sue Bloxham and Mike Heathfield

INTRODUCTION

The ability to study in a more autonomous and independent way is one of the key student competences promoted by government-sponsored initiatives such as the Improving Student Learning Project and Enterprise in Higher Education. These initiatives seem to be driven by, among other things, the ever-present concern for improved productivity, the influence of educational psychology, and the technicist concerns of government policy (Furlong and Maynard, 1995).

This chapter reports on a study of small-scale innovation in the context of a course designed to provide a post-experience, professional qualification in community and youth work. Critical professional learning describes both the intended style of learning and its purposes. The chapter identifies the assumptions that underpin the development, briefly describing the course, the research methodology and relevant parts of the research results, and discusses the findings in the light of appropriate educational theory. We focus on the element of the research results which identified some specific difficulties experienced by students; we discuss these as the interesting, but unexpected, consequences of the learning innovations.

Improving student learning in higher education (HE) has been the focus of both research and staff development for a number of years (Biggs, 1989; Eley, 1992; Entwistle and Ramsden, 1983; Gibbs, 1992a) with a reasonably consistent body of research suggesting that students' approach to learning is influenced by aspects of the learning context with particular features encouraging a 'meaning orientation' amongst students (see also Chapter 10).

A weakness of existing research is that sophisticated models of student learning (Biggs, 1989; Entwistle, 1987; Ramsden, 1992) have drawn much of their evidence from studies of students operating in fairly traditional academic environments. There is now a considerable and growing range of examples of developing practice (Gibbs, 1992b; Ramsden, 1992). However, research on courses designed to promote deep learning strategies has indicated that this success is not universal and that some students do not adapt their learning style in tune with the course requirements. In part, this is explained by the notion of students having an incorrect perception of what is required (Marton and Saljo, 1984), but in other cases, students behaved in a way contrary to their own views of the course demands (Eley, 1992). Therefore, there is clearly a gap in our understanding of how students interact with innovative teaching methods. Ramsden (1992) argues that 'deep approaches are fragile things; while we can create favourable conditions for them, students' previous experience *and other unmeasured factors* may mean that they remain unexercised' (p.80, emphasis added).

A key underlying feature of the innovation described in this chapter was an attempt to utilize research on learning context in designing a course that would encourage such a deep approach (the details will follow). The course concerned was a one-year vocational programme for graduates seeking to become qualified as youth and community workers, so there was a strong professional element to the course design. Professional training has suffered even more scrutiny and pressure than the purely academic elements of HE, with the growing intervention of many stakeholders including government, professional bodies, employers and practitioners. Not surprisingly, models of professional training are in constant flux with open and frequently savage debate about, for example, the respective merits of competency approaches, reflective approaches, and about the roles of HE and of the agencies in which students practise. The course was designed to develop reflective practitioners in the wider context of a 'social reconstructionist' tradition. Such a tradition is concerned to produce professionals who play a positive role in the making of a more just, equitable and humane society, where technical proficiency is valued but only for its ability to achieve desired ends (Zeichner and Teitelbaum, 1982), notably that of social justice. This involves a clear recognition of the value-base of both the curriculum and the pedagogy in striving for radical practice (Gore, 1993). There are resonances of this approach in Grundy's use of Habermas' concept of 'emancipatory interest' as a basis for critical curriculum practice; a curriculum identified with the development of autonomy and responsibility, justice and equality (Grundy, 1987).

While both the assumptions of 'reflection' and 'social reconstructionism' are subject to considerable debate (Furlong and Maynard, 1995), they are beyond the scope of this chapter. Knowledge of this background is, however, essential in providing a context for the methodology of the research and for interpreting student reactions. It is also important to recognize that, unlike many teacher education settings (Gore, 1993; Gore and Zeichner, 1991), the assumptions of social reconstructionism are not marginal to community and youth work but are a fundamental part of the professional culture.

THE INNOVATION: CRITICAL PROFESSIONAL LEARNING

The course (at least ostensibly) had been radically reshaped to meet the following higher-order aims, derived from the assumptions discussed above:

- To improve the quality of learning during the course and to encourage the development of lifelong effective learners.

- To improve the quality of professional practice demonstrated by students during and on completion of the course.

- To develop practitioners with a commitment to critical, emancipatory practice and change.

These higher-order aims translated, for us, into a set of principles to guide the course design and teaching. These were the drive for:

- Deep learning (Biggs, 1989). This was to be fostered by an effort to create more autonomous, self-directed learners. It called for a decreased dependency on the authority and knowledge of tutors, and required opportunities for learning which involved activity and interaction, enhanced motivation, were characterized by a clear structure, and employed problem-based learning methods.

- Students to develop a clear philosophy/purpose for their professional work which included the mission of social justice. This was to be fostered by the use of learning groups as critical communities (Grundy, 1987); by exercises and research activities aimed at helping learners to develop a philosophy of community and youth work; and by appropriate curriculum tasks and materials.

- Students to develop a coherent professional identity. This was to be fostered by a programme that simulated the demands of professional practice; that gave opportunities for responsibility and autonomy; and that provided opportunities for action, and for structured reflection and feedback, as well as giving opportunities to practise skills.

In attempting to meet these objectives, the new course involved setting students a range of tasks and problems which could only be resolved through independent research, working in learning groups, sharing information and experiences, negotiating between themselves, and seeking ideas and information from tutors, agencies, current professionals and, of course, from the library. Traditional teaching was largely replaced by tutor-produced problems and resource materials, with taught sessions focusing on practical skills and introductions to key ideas. The tasks were designed in an holistic way in order to help students develop an understanding of the underlying structure of the subject matter as well as advancing its integration into professional practice. Teaching hours were reduced by 40 per cent but the overall student programme was designed to replicate the workload and requirements for personal organization that would be experienced in a full-time youth and community work post. Detailed examples of the assessment tasks can be found in Bloxham and Heathfield (1994). We shall refer to this composite model of course design as 'critical professional learning'.

THE RESEARCH

The research on this innovation has taken place over two years with two different cohorts of students. In each case the research sample involved two-thirds of the student group of approximately 18 students. The overall group profile for students on this course over the two years of the research was two-thirds female. Slightly over half of each cohort were aged between 21 and 25 with the remainder spread between 26 and the late 30s. The groups were largely of a white ethnic background with one Asian student in each year. A small group in both years was from Northern Ireland. The students had largely graduated with degrees in the social sciences, humanities or performing arts and had received second class degrees in approximately four-fifths of cases with the last fifth having received third class degrees. They came from a range of universities and polytechnics. A requirement for entry in all cases was voluntary or paid experience in a youth and community work setting sufficient to demonstrate an aptitude for the work.

In the first year, the sample of 12 students was chosen to reflect a cross-section of student responses to the ASQ (see Gibbs, 1992a) adminis-tered during the course. Each of these students was interviewed in the final term of the course by an independent interviewer. Data were analysed by a content analysis of the transcripts. Overall, the research results from the first cohort confirmed the general results of existing research on the impact of innovative and independence-based courses, including the finding that while a positive outcome of the innovation was observed for the majority, a minority of students failed to benefit fully from the experiences we had devised.

It was as though the learning design provided the right conditions for deep learning and the development of effective practitioners with a commit-ment to critical practice, but only for those students who were able to take advantage of it. The research indicated that approximately a quarter of the respondents struggled with the learning context; they contested the notion of student-directed activity and lost motivation as the course progressed. The sample was too small for the figure itself to be more than indicative of the existence of a pool of such students.

The research with the second cohort continued the qualitative approach of our first project. It involved semi-structured interviews with two-thirds of the students (12) in the 1993/4 cohort. The students volunteered to take part. Interviews were conducted by an independent interviewer (not part of the course team or department) at the beginning of the year, after one term, and near the end of the last term. Each interview covered new material regarding the student and their progress on and experience of the course, but interviews also included a number of repeated questions relating to aspects of the course content. These latter questions were included to detect changes in the students' understanding over the course of the year. Interviews were supplemented by material from an end-of-year course team discussion and evaluation which focused on the course design and its impact on student approaches to learning, and the quality of the learning itself.

While not making any claims as to the representativeness of the interview material, it clearly delineates student perceptions, feelings and understandings related to the course experience. Likewise our interpretation of these responses is not value-free.

The second analytical stage was designed to explore the interaction between student differences, the learning context and student outcomes. Therefore it was necessary to categorize the research participants according to whether they appeared to have benefited from the course and its design. This categorization was carried out according to whether:

(a) the student demonstrated learning of 'relational' and 'extended abstract' nature in answer to questions regarding course content (Biggs, 1989);
(b) the student felt confident to start work in the field of community and youth work;
(c) the student's views were compatible with the general design of the course, particularly exhibiting a critical and personal engagement with the curriculum.

In keeping with the qualitative nature of the study, categorization of each student's individual experience involved a combination of all three criteria. This process, conducted independently by the two tutor/researchers, produced six students (50 per cent) who were considered to have had a very beneficial experience (benefiting students). The other six students were considered not to have benefited fully (non-benefiting students) and two of them seemed to have had a considerable struggle with the course pedagogy. As with the first year's findings, these proportions cannot be considered representative of a wider population but merely indicate the existence of different groups of students.

RESULTS

Analysis of the research data has enabled us to develop a number of hypotheses regarding the interaction of the various elements considered to contribute to student learning. For the purposes of this chapter, we are concentrating on hypotheses related to the learning context, although other results were related to student difference. Clearly, the scale of this research enables us only to present some tentative ideas regarding the problems posed by critical professional learning methods. The hope is that the study shows the need for a move from research on the general effects of independence-based methods to research into the specific issues raised by student' experience of those methods.

Departmental background

Trigwell and Prosser (1991) make the point that innovations at the level of the individual teacher will not necessarily be successful if they are not supported and complemented across the school or department. One satisfying aspect of this course is that it takes place in a department where there is managerial support, appropriate assessment schedules, and all the staff teaching the course are in sympathy with the direction of the changes. However, being in general sympathy with the direction of critical professional learning may not actually mean that tutors' teaching and assessment are based on the underlying assumptions described above, nor that they are perceived to be so by the students. It may be the case that students are not getting a consistent message, are confused by different demands, or are not being offered sufficient structure to link the different course units together.

Indeed, it was interesting to discover that the students' perceptions of different units of the course varied considerably, regardless of whether they were benefiting or non-benefiting students. While this is not surprising in itself, given that the units had different tutors, it is surprising in that a number of students complained that some courses had not had as much teaching as others, when in fact all units had had similar contact time. Analysis of the data suggests that students equated teaching with the clarity of the framework that was provided to help them learn, rather than with the actual amount of contact with a tutor. Therefore, where tutors had altered their contact time in order to use it primarily to set up, monitor and evaluate independent and group learning tasks, students were happier with the teaching time devoted to the unit. Where tutors had tried to squeeze their normal amount of teaching input into reduced contact hours with additional assignments, students felt that they had insufficient teaching and demonstrated less active personal engagement with the content. There is a message here regarding the development of innovative pedagogy. It cannot be done without almost going back to the first principles of the course and rethinking how the various learning outcomes can be met in a more open way. Tinkering with existing courses may satisfy no one. Trigwell *et al.*'s (1994) work on lecturers' intentions suggests that change in teaching techniques will only follow where there is a complementary change in intention on the part of the tutor: 'As long as teaching staff hold transmission intentions in teaching, suggesting student focused strategies will be a futile and misunderstood pursuit' (p.83). Therefore, it may be the case that some staff involved in the programme reported here have a general sympathy with increasing levels of student activity and interaction, but have, in practice, retained elements of 'teacher focus' and information transmission. This may indicate the need for provision of a strong theoretical base for staff development in a course designed with critical professional learning as the outcome. Providing lots of examples of techniques will be insufficient if tutors do not demonstrate sufficient understanding for an appropriate change in intention to occur. In the case of our notion of critical professional learning, this change in intention must be accompanied by a fundamental review of the foundations of the content and process of the pedagogy.

Workload

A perceived heavy workload has been shown to drive students towards a reproducing orientation (Gibbs, 1992a; Trigwell and Prosser, 1991). Ramsden (1992) argues that courses with excessive content are so demanding of student time that little space remains for the essential activities of understanding and integrating the content:

> The inevitable result of too much busy work is that many students adopt minimising strategies and complete their courses with sketchy and confused knowledge of the topics they have 'learned'. (Ramsden, 1992, p.138)

We wanted our course to simulate a professional workload and some of the stresses of self-organization and team work. Yet we were recruiting a proportion of our students from undergraduate courses where, with strategic study practices (and a lot of work before finals), students would have been able to limit their time commitment. It is interesting that there appears to be a strong match between students who had recently completed their degrees (within the last 12 months) and those who were categorized as non-benefiting. Those who had finished their undergraduate education earlier and had established themselves in full-time work appeared more likely to benefit from the course, as Table 5.1 shows.

Clearly the figures are too small to be statistically significant and there may be other factors at work, such as levels of motivation and maturity, or the dramatic change in teaching context faced by those who had just completed largely traditional HE courses. Nevertheless, the amount of work involved in our course may have created an unexpected demand on students as yet unused to the workload associated with full-time posts.

Furthermore, the issue of excessive student workload may be a more general feature of independence-based methods. As Keats and Boughey (1994) state in discussing a similar innovation:

> Under the standard lecture approach, students are expected to study a given quantity of material, but there are few checks that they actually do the work. With this method, there are built-in checks, and students may perceive this as extra work. (p.72)

The course design assumed that students are assessment-driven and therefore tried to ensure that all the planned learning outcomes were built into assessment items. The assessment tasks were designed to encourage students to understand the materials, validate them (or not) in their professional context and make them their own. With more conventional courses, where assessment tends to allow students to select only parts of a subject for investigation (for example, two essay topics and three or four topics for the exam), they are able to limit their workload. By ensuring that everything is assessed, we effectively extended the curriculum by 50 per cent or more as there were no parts that students could ignore.

Table 5.1 *Course outcomes and student experience*

	Just finished degree	**Established in full-time work**	**Total**
Benefiting students	1	5	6
Non-benefiting students	4	2	6
Total	5	7	12

The research reported here certainly indicates that students, whether categorized as benefiting or non-benefiting, were deeply unhappy with the amount of work that they had to do. Of greater concern was the view expressed by two-thirds of the students that the quantity of work had affected the quality of learning:

> This term I've been most motivated when I've approached these things how I want to do them. But now I've just got so much to do. Part of that is perhaps lacking motivation that I haven't got on with it, but I just know that I haven't got the time to spend doing the sort of standard of work I want to do, so I'm not particularly motivated about it (subject 5).

> But it feels a lot like it's just like get the work in really and the deeper learning which is so vital is like missed or skimmed over... the work is there to do, it brings up issues and then we've got another piece of work to do so you just like push it to one side. And I think things are like superficially being learned but not being learnt deep down (subject 4).

On this basis, independence-based methods appear to increase significantly the experienced curriculum rather than merely change the form of its delivery. One possible conclusion is that course design for independent study will require a significant reduction in the quantity of curriculum content if it is intended to safeguard the promotion of a meaning orientation in students' approach to learning and to provide opportunities for critical, personal reflection. Perhaps this reduction should be considered in the light of the amount of learning that students on traditional courses are said to actually retain once their examinations are over:

What I'm learning, it's like staying in, it's not going and leaving me, which at university I think it did. It was there and it would be gone again. It would be like... it wasn't there any more (subject 3).

However, in the case of vocational courses such as ours, the option to reduce the curriculum may be closed; external professional bodies require accredited courses to cover large areas of predetermined content. There is an important job for HE staff in educating professional bodies to rewrite their accreditation requirements in terms of key concepts and skills rather than significant amounts of knowledge. Recent research with employers of graduates could provide supporting evidence for a reduction in subject content (Harvey with Green, 1994).

A further aspect of workload is that the level of personal engagement that is always likely to be there is heightened by the very nature of critical professional learning methods, thereby adding to the intensity of the course:

I knew it was going to be hard but I didn't think it would be quite this hard – not just the physical workload but the amount of head space you have to give it all the time, and it's just the stress of it all (subject 5).

For me it's everyday life. For me like... I mean it's the whole thing... I think you can't have theory without practice, practice without theory. For me... it's part of me, it's everything that I do, like relates to... (subject 3).

My sensitivity to stuff is really heightened and like I don't even realize I'm doing it, but I'm assessing things all the time, whether it's accessible and stuff like that (subject 4).

Students recognized that the emotional intensity of the course was affected by the way that the processes of critical professional learning entailed interaction with others:

Well I mean it's stressful in a lot of ways because it's... the issues that we're dealing with are stressful, so I mean people come with their own agendas, their own hurts, their own things that they feel strongly about. There's also... the workload is extremely stressful because there is an awful lot of work, but I think the workload in itself is not the total be-all of the stress, I think it's a combination of factors. One of them is the fact that we do a lot of work in groups and... I think the issues that we're dealing with (subject 10).

CONCLUSION

The link between the results seen here and other similar studies discussed above suggests that there is a clear need for further research regarding students' experiences of innovative learning environments and the development of independent study methods.

Conclusions, replicated elsewhere, indicate that staff need to pay attention to a series of important factors if the benefits of new forms of teaching are successfully going to reach a broader range of students. The central ones covered in this study are:

- Independence-based course designs need to be supported by a clear philosophy and rationale which has the full understanding and sympathy of the staff involved in teaching it. The translation of the philosophy of independent learning into the specific details of course delivery and assessment demands a high level of commitment and involvement from all concerned.

- Courses which seek actively to engage students with the whole curriculum need a circumspect selection (and reduction) of course content to avoid excessive workload forcing students into a 'reproducing' mode of learning at the expense of the reflection which appears so crucial to the intended process.

- A goal of innovation is that students actively engage with the material and identify meaning for themselves. However, the sense of success with this programme must be tempered by a recognition that such a high level of engagement is associated with stress, which can also work against the programme's aims.

Chapter 6

Learning from experience: an individually negotiated learning route

Peter Funnell and Sharon Goddard

INTRODUCING INDEPENDENT STUDY

The Suffolk College is a large 'mixed economy' adult, further and higher education college with some 7,000 full-time equivalent learners of whom approximately 3,000 are higher education learners (1994/95 figures). The college is, with the exception of the Open University, the only significant provider of higher education in the county of Suffolk and is an Associate college of the University of East Anglia, the only college with this status. Higher education provision has grown significantly in the college since 1988, reflecting the strong desire of the college staff, governing body, and more recently college corporation, and the local community to expand higher education opportunities locally, regionally and where appropriate nationally in line with the vocational strengths of the college. The provision of courses by Independent Study (IS) franchised from the then Polytechnic of East London (PEL), and offered on a part-time basis, were an important component of this development.

The decision to franchise IS and to fund the significant programme of staff development which supported its introduction was based on a number of clear premises:

- that higher education by IS would be an attractive style of learning for adult learners resident in the local community who wished to study on a part-time basis;

- that a form of study based on learner-devised learning contracts would be an effective means of identifying and meeting learner needs;

- that meeting the anticipated diversity of learner needs would best enable higher education teaching and learning to be undertaken across the whole institution;

- that the innovative teaching, learning and assessment strategies which IS would introduce into the college would themselves act as valuable agents of change.

Significantly, IS also built on the traditional strengths of the further education sector, namely an emphasis on developing learner capability through the acquisition and demonstration of 'core' employability skills and a commitment to teaching and the facilitation of learning over competing priorities such as research activity. Indeed, elements of the philosophy of IS had been promulgated through state-driven initiatives such as the Technical and Vocational Education Initiative (TVEI) and projects sponsored by the Work Related Further Education Development Fund and the Further Education Unit.

The first cohort of Dip HE learners was recruited in September 1989 and a full undergraduate programme was introduced in 1990, providing an opportunity for learners to enter directly into level 3 of the programme based on the accreditation of their prior learning.

A core of personal tutors was recruited and led by a programme leader who was charged with managing the programme and providing academic consultancy to individual learners. Each learner was also supported by a 'subject-specialist' tutor from the appropriate discipline area with a second 'specialist' being identified from amongst PEL staff or elsewhere as appropriate. Quality assurance issues were shared by the two institutions with a 'phase one' assessment board meeting at Suffolk College with results submitted to the main, 'phase two' IS assessment board at PEL.

The college was attracted by the approach to education for capability represented by IS (Stephenson and Laycock, 1993), especially by the value that IS places on individualized learner-centred education, which represented a tangible expression of the college's wish to be increasingly proactive in identifying and meeting learner needs. In this sense IS clearly reflected the institution's commitment to providing learners with an environment offering accessibility, choice, relevance, progression and support. Particular importance was attached to the development of each learner's personal effectiveness, learning competence and developing ability to reflect critically on learning. Moreover, both TVEI and the delivery of learning funded through training credits put a premium on facilitative styles and processes mirrored by IS. Finally, the value IS places on educational guidance and its particular approach to tutoring reflects and extends curriculum debate and practice within further education.

In this context IS in the 'mixed economy' environment of Suffolk College was, and continues to be, seen as both informing and being informed by the different traditions, contexts, issues and themes of further and higher education. It was recognized at an early stage that the introduction of IS would require a considerable initial programme of staff development. In practice this consisted of three sub-programmes: one provided for the initial DipHE personal tutorial team; a wider programme to support undergraduate 'generalist' tutoring; and a third for subject-specialist tutors. Recruitment of staff to the programme was, in large part, through self-selection, with interested staff participating in a series of introductory events. At the end of this process a group of staff emerged who undertook extensive and intensive staff development to enable them to become IS tutors. The staff development programme was drawn up by PEL staff in consultation with intended tutors at the college. The approach for personal tutors was experiential, with staff producing their own learning contracts to plan their development as personal tutors. In addition, seminars were held on key issues such as the structure, philosophy and operation of IS, and college staff visited PEL, becoming members of tutor groups, participating in learners' workshop programmes and course committee meetings.

The role of the personal tutor was identified as essential to the successful delivery of IS. Wheeler and Birtle (1993) have defined a personal tutor as an academic member of staff whose role may include the following responsibilities:

- to facilitate the personal development of their tutees

- to monitor the progress of their tutees

- to provide a link between the learner and the university authorities

- to be a responsible adult... in whom the learner can confide

- to intervene with the university authorities on behalf of their tutees. (p.15)

However, IS personal tutors were also to be responsible for developing an academic programme of study with their learners and for enabling them to monitor and evaluate their achievement of learning goals. This significantly extended the usual tutorial role and placed the relationship between the tutor and tutee at the forefront of the learning process.

The location of the management of the IS initiative was also recognized to be an important consideration. It was recognized that a criticism of initiatives such as IS is that they can leave teaching staff isolated from their subject discipline. This concern was addressed by locating the management of the initiative and the central team of personal tutors in the college's central curriculum programmes unit, with subject specialists 'serviced' from staff within faculties. This structure was designed to support strong programme management while retaining the professional and academic integrity of specialist staff who would work across a number of courses and programmes within their subject or discipline area.

REFLECTIONS ON IS AT THE SUFFOLK COLLEGE

The IS initiative has made a significant contribution to institutional change and been particularly valuable in:

- providing opportunities for learners to build upon existing knowledge and expertise;

- providing opportunities for learners to negotiate their curriculum with personal and specialist tutors within a challenging educational environment;

- encouraging facilitative and mutually respectful relationships between staff and learners;

- encouraging learners and staff to work in central interdisciplinary groups, where experience both in the content and processes of higher education can be shared across traditional subject boundaries;

- providing a curriculum entitlement characterized by the development of supporting and contextual studies. This has proved particularly appropriate for mature learners returning to study.

The emphasis on learner empowerment through negotiation of both curriculum and assessment has also instigated debate within the institution about the direction and form of higher education provision during a period of significant change both within Suffolk College and in higher education provision nationally. Indeed, at a macro level, it has been argued that changes in the nature of higher education represent a crisis generating uncertainty about how institutions can rise to the challenge of changed funding arrangements, quality enhancement and employer expectations (see, for example, Ainley, 1994). The IS initiative and its unique approach to learning have positively and professionally supported the institution in addressing some of these issues. However, it would be misleading to suggest that the IS initiative has not had its critics. Indeed, through such criticism a number of important curriculum issues have emerged, leading to an extended review and reconsideration of the initiative and subsequent reformulation of the product. It is interesting to note that a similar process of redesign was occurring concurrently at PEL (O'Reilly, 1993).

One of the most significant issues arose from the mode of delivery. Since IS was offered solely on a part-time basis, it had been anticipated that learners would either be planning unique programmes of study related to their employment or be using it to enable them to change career direction. This proved not to be the case. With experience it became clear that learners were often entering higher education from non-standard educational backgrounds and were keen to participate in general subject-based group sessions. However, as IS encouraged interdisciplinary, and occasionally esoteric, choices of subject area, there were often occasions when a corresponding college course of an appropriate level did not exist, or was not available because of timetabling constraints.

Given this, it emerged that far from being offered a wider choice of teaching and learning strategies, IS learners were increasingly being directed into solitary and largely book-based 'finding out' activities, which appeared, on occasion, to constrain rather than support learner development. This was particularly so for learners who were not in employment and who were not, therefore, trying to resolve a work-based issue. Within this solitary type of learning, some learners experienced great difficulty in using the academic language of their subject area since there were limited opportunities for them to debate issues and dilemmas, ideas and insights with other learners who shared a subject interest. More generally, learners tended to become over-focused and specialized, and experienced difficulty in relating their programme of study to a broader subject context.

In discussions with staff and learners there emerged a recognition that a more structured framework for, and access to, academic learning support was essential. For most learners entering at level 1, a whole programme based on independent learning principles was judged to be inappropriate. Rather, a mixture of learning strategies including taught elements and a course structure which progressively developed learner autonomy, was seen as likely to enhance the learners' experiences, while the development of full-time provision offered alongside redesigned part-time provision would maximize learning opportunities. These reflections on practice informed the development of the successor to IS at the college introduced in September 1993: the Individually Negotiated Learning Route (INLR) through the Suffolk Modular Degree Programme (SMDP). This programme was a response to the national drive towards modular and credit accumulation and transfer schemes in higher education, coupled with a local desire to offer flexible, broad-based programmes of study. It is a pan-institutional, centrally managed, modular scheme which encompasses the majority of the college's undergraduate provision.

The INLR replaces the IS initiative and seeks to redress many of the curriculum issues previously identified. It enables learners to combine taught modules with self-directed elements of study delivered through a learning contract. Perhaps the most innovative aspect of any modular scheme lies in the potential for learner choice and particularly for the choice of unusual or non-traditional combinations of study. However, the extent to which such unusual combinations are actually permitted within the practice of modular schemes rests largely with the academic subject gate-keepers and with the intended or unintended constraints of choice consequent upon a complex network of pre- and co-requisites for enrolment on modules. INLR challenges these subject boundaries by prescribing a pattern of study which encourages learners to plan broad-based study at level 1, and then to progressively take responsibility for their learning by designing and carrying out individual research and study at levels 2 and 3 (see Figure 6.1). These pieces of individual work enable learners to negotiate their choice of subject matter, learning and research methods and learning outcomes. As such the INLR responds to the earlier criticism of IS in the Suffolk context both by structuring learner choice into the programme and by making full and explicit use of the modules available elsewhere in the SMDP.

Underpinning the design of the INLR is a belief that, as active participants in the learning process, learners gain in motivation and personal development. This approach is characterized by a problem-solving methodology through which learners formulate and tackle problems within their discipline area. However, acknowledging the earlier review of the IS initiative, the INLR has been designed to recognize that independent capability is strengthened if learners have a secure grounding in the principles and methodologies of their academic subject area. Consequently the self-directed learning elements of the INLR become more prominent as the learners progress through the programme, enabling them to benefit from membership of a subject-based community within the taught subject modules at levels 1 and 2.

The process and research modules available at all levels of study within the INLR seek to develop each learner's capability through a structured approach to critical self-evaluation, the identification of learning goals, the planning and monitoring of progress, and critical reflection on learning. Recognizing the possibility that any modular programme may present a fragmented learning experience, these process modules require the learner to reflect upon, and justify, the coherence of the chosen programme of study. Thus the choice of modules and research topics rests with the learner as, ultimately, does the coherence of the individual programme of study. Evidence of level 1 learners' perceptions suggests that the new format is creating a more structured opportunity to develop individual capability while offering a grounding in traditional subject-based knowledge and methodology. However, this will remain a matter for continuous quality audit and review and amendments will be introduced as necessary to safeguard the essential principles of learner choice and empowerment.

There is a tension, even in a 'mixed economy' institution, between more traditional tutor-designed academic programmes and those constructed by learners. In particular, issues of coherence and appropriateness in learner-designed higher education beg questions about academic ownership, quality, standards and comparability. Such challenges, which permeate the higher education sector, are compounded in 'mixed economy' contexts where institutions are subject to multiple peer inspection and scrutiny from validating partners and external examiners as well as the Further Education Funding Council, Higher Education Funding Council and Higher Education Quality Council.

This tension raises issues about the professional role of academics and about the notion that they are definers and custodians of a legitimate body of knowledge, skills and capabilities which define programmes of study and levels of achievement. Equally, students themselves can be resistant to taking ownership of their programmes since this requires a considerable (and potentially unsettling) leap in confidence and competence and can involve them in confronting their own conservatism as well as that of academic staff (Baume, 1994).

For learners who do achieve this leap, the rewards in motivation, quality of academic performance and in personal development can be considerable. The idea that self-education, or knowledge as self-production, is the only knowledge that really matters is a concept at the centre of the design of the INLR. As such the approach to learning on the INLR can be seen to be part of a continuum of radical approaches to education which have sought to empower and transform individuals and which are essentially oppositional to established practice. This curriculum represents one point of balance between content and process models of education, hence between different positions in the continuing debate about the purpose of higher education.

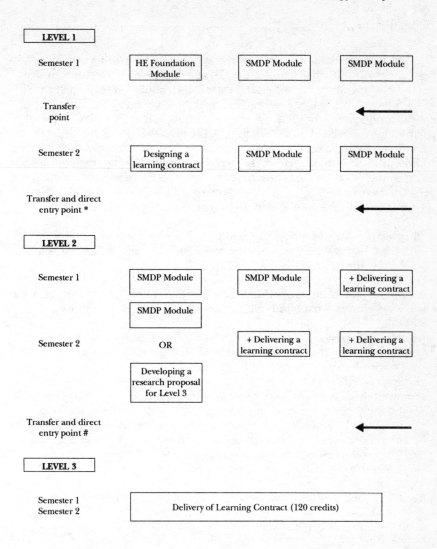

Notes: All modules are valued at 20 credits unless separately specified.

* Transfer or direct entry to Level 2 is only possible upon successful completion of the Level 1 module 'Designing a learning contract'.
+ Delivering a learning contract' at Level 2 is a 60 credit module taken over two semesters.
# Transfer or direct entry to Level 3 is only possible upon successful completion of the Level 2 module 1 'Developing a Research Proposal for Level 3'.

Figure 6.1 *Structure of the individually negotiated learning route*

CONCLUSION

The INLR represents one institution's attempt to offer innovative educational opportunities in an area of the UK which experiences relative under-provision of higher education. It is an attempt to hold firm to the principles of IS while mirroring more closely the needs and aspirations of learners. As a new product, the INLR reflects many of the characteristics of the IS programmes offered elsewhere in the UK (Brook, 1993; Hodgkinson, 1993). As a piece of educational practice it has been designed to support learners through a transformatory process in which the individual increasingly takes ownership of his or her learning. This emphasis on transformation has been associated with a notion of 'value-addedness' as a hallmark of quality provision. In this view, the role of educational providers is to ensure:

> that learners fully participate in, and contribute to, the learning process in such a way that they become responsible for creating, delivering and evaluating the product. (Brook, 1993, p.175)

This notion has been taken further by Barnett (1992) who promotes a learner-centred approach to higher education. For Barnett:

> it is the learner who primarily does the achieving. Teachers, laboratories, computers, resources in general, and the total paraphernalia of institutions are secondary to this end. Students have to give something of themselves if they are to engage authentically with the experiences that confront them. It is to be hoped that the institutional framework will have a positive effect in assisting this process.... Forming an understanding, making a statement, offering evidence, drawing conclusions, making an inference or producing an insight into or a solution to a problem: it is the learner's own personal involvement in these acts... that is indicative of a genuinely higher education. (p.203)

The INLR, itself a product of experiential learning, seeks to offer such a higher education.

Chapter 7

Action-centred learning in industry

Richard Carter, Frank Cooke and Bob Neal

INTRODUCTION

The MSc course in engineering project management at Lancaster University had its origin in a need, on the part of one company, for a course to teach experienced, high-flying, engineers the skills needed to manage project teams. The target student group comprised engineers qualified to degree or to HNC/HND level, who were identified by their employers as potential project managers or team leaders. These students were typically 25 to 35 years old and many had some years of responsible experience in a technical role, and family commitments. They were highly motivated but did not normally have recent experience of university study. The challenge was, therefore, to design a course which could promote effective learning of a range of skills for students who could not be spared from their jobs for long periods at a time and who would need to combine study with the demands of those jobs and of their personal lives.

The course has been developed jointly by the authors who brought to the task the different traditions and methods of academia and industrial training (Carter and Cooke, 1987). The synthesis of these two approaches has produced a course which combines the academic emphasis on depth of knowledge and sound argument with the industrial experience of action learning. During the ten years of the course's existence there have been a number of changes:

- the typical age range of the students is now 35 to 45 years

- the seniority of the posts held by the students has increased dramatically, and

- the duration and content of the taught modules is different.

But the objectives and the educational approach have remained the same throughout. The fact that the course has proved attractive to students and their employers from a wide range of industries, while changing very little from the original conception, is a clear indication of the success of the approach adopted.

AIMS AND OBJECTIVES

It was decided from the outset that the aim of the course should be to develop the students into competent managers of both themselves and their projects. The objectives were therefore specified in terms of the skills which they should possess and be able to demonstrate, by the end of the course. It was found that it was best to define the objectives in rather general terms with the expectation that each might be satisfied in a variety of ways according to the learning environment of each student. Thus, on completion of the course, successful students must have demonstrated, in an industrial and commercial context, the ability to:

● define tasks

● generate ideas

● make and justify decisions

● plan and control activities

● evaluate the results of activities

● communicate effectively

● work effectively with people

● continue personal development.

It will be observed that these objectives bear a close resemblance to the aspects of problem-solving as described by Koberg and Bagnall (1981). This is not accidental because industrial project management requires well-developed problem-solving skills and each project can itself be regarded as a problem to be solved. It should also be noted that the requirement to demonstrate competence in an industrial and commercial context implied that every student must undertake a project in industry for which he or she has full managerial responsibility. The last objective indicates the importance which is placed upon the students' ownership of the learning process. The course therefore has the subsidiary aim that the students should become excited by the possibilities opened up by learning and should want to carry on learning after the course has ended.

It is considered important that these objectives are stated explicitly at the start of the course and that all assessment is carried out against them. The achievement of the aims of the course requires that the students should not merely be taught a range of techniques for project management, but that they should be assisted to develop into people who use good practices habitually. These educational objectives can be understood in terms of the taxonomy of objectives for professional education shown in Table 7.1 (Carter, 1985).

Table 7.1 *A taxonomy of objectives for professional education*

MENTAL CHARACTERISTICS	ATTITUDES AND VALUES	PERSONALITY CHARACTERISTICS	SPIRITUAL QUALITIES
Openness Agility Imagination Creativity	Things Self People Groups Ideas	Integrity Initiative Industry Emotional resilience	Appreciation Response
MENTAL SKILLS	**INFORMATION SKILLS**	**ACTION SKILLS**	**SOCIAL SKILLS**
Organization Analysis Evaluation Synthesis	Acquisition Recording Remembering Communication	Manual Organizing Decision-making Problem-solving	Cooperation Leadership Negotiation and persuasion Interviewing
FACTUAL KNOWLEDGE		**EXPERIENTIAL KNOWLEDGE**	
Facts Structures Procedures Concepts Principles		Experience Internalization Generalization Abstraction	

The course objectives are drawn almost entirely from the skills in the second level of the table, while being underpinned by detailed knowledge at the first level. A fundamental difference between skills and knowledge, as defined here, is that skills can be possessed at different levels of competence and can be improved by practice. Thus the decision to frame the main objectives in terms of skills led naturally to an educational approach which emphasized the need to practise the skills and to learn from both success and failure. In other words, the choice of experiential learning as the course methodology was implicit in the specification of skill objectives.

The aims of the course, however, go beyond the acquisition of a set of independent skills. A good project manager must be able to employ all these skills in relationship to one another and competence requires the development of *metaskills* of this kind (Burgoyne and Stuart, 1976). This development implies change in and development of the personal qualities described in the third, upper level of Table 7.1. These qualities are deeply rooted and change only slowly, but we have found that quite dramatic changes have occurred in our students' outlook on life as a result of participation in the course.

COURSE STRUCTURE

The course comprises eight one-week modules of intensive teaching at the university and a major, industrially based, project. In the modules the students are introduced to the key skills they will need through workshop sessions. They are also made aware of the corpus of relevant knowledge so that they can follow up particular themes by independent study during the rest of the year. The workshop-style teaching emphasizes student participation and sharing of existing knowledge, and the teacher is the facilitator of learning rather than a dispenser of received wisdom *ex cathedra*. The first module concentrates on the development of the students' learning and problem-solving skills. In this way it provides an introduction to university postgraduate study and to the educational approach used throughout the course. The first six modules are arranged in pairs occupying consecutive weeks with gaps of about four weeks between them. The remaining two modules take place later in the course and provide an opportunity for coverage of topics specifically requested by the students.

During the first six modules a rôle play, known as the linking project, is undertaken by the students in groups. This project provides them with the opportunity to apply in a safe situation, some of the skills they have learnt. Mistakes can be made, analysed and learnt from without the fear of the consequences which would be involved in a real project. The linking project culminates in group presentations to a 'client' and in individual reports on the process aspects (the 'how' and 'why') of the project and of what has been learnt from it. It therefore serves as an introduction to, and demonstration of, the methods of experiential learning which are emphasized throughout the course.

The students carry out individual main projects in their employing organizations over a period of 12 to 18 months. The main project provides the chief source of learning as each student grapples with the problems which it poses day by day and shares these experiences with other members of the 'set' group. It is, however, made clear to the students that they should regard their whole lives as sources of learning opportunities throughout the period of the course.

SUPPORT FOR LEARNING

The experiential learning process is supported in a number of interrelated ways. Key among these is the use of peer support (set) groups (Lessem, 1984). These groups have a fixed membership of up to six students and meet about once every six weeks during the course. The membership of the groups is chosen to produce the greatest possible range of educational and professional backgrounds. Students from the same company are never placed in the same group if it can possibly be avoided. The aim of the groups is to aid each student's learning and self-development through mutual encouragement, criticism and sharing of ideas. It is essential that the group members trust each other because the groups can only work effectively if the members can be open with each other about themselves. The discussions of the group are therefore treated as confidential to the group members. It is normal for an action learning set group to be supported by a set adviser whose function is to facilitate the formation of the group and to assist it in achieving its objectives (Casey, 1983). Our usual practice is to employ two advisers, one drawn from the university, the other from industry. We have found that this is a particularly effective technique. We regard it as very important that the advisers should always be seen as the friends and supporters of the members of their groups. For this reason they never undertake any summative assessment of the members of their own groups. For the same reason we try to avoid placing industrial advisers with groups containing students from their own companies.

The group advisers who are university staff members act as tutors to the members of their groups. They discuss each student's progress and comment in detail upon the work produced for formative assessment either within the set group or individually.

Each student is encouraged to keep a daily process diary to act as a record of thoughts and feelings about the events of the day (Rainer, 1980). This diary is regarded as a confidential document which is never inspected by tutors though it may, on occasion, be shown to them voluntarily. The most important function of the diary is to encourage reflection on events as part of the experiential learning cycle. It also provides source material for formative assessment and for the final dissertation.

ASSESSMENT

The assessment of the students' performance is achieved by requiring them to write a number of reports and a final dissertation, and to make two oral presentations. The proportions of the final summative assessment derived from each are indicated in parentheses below.

At the conclusion of the linking project each group prepares a report and makes a formal presentation of it to the 'client' (10 per cent). Each student subsequently writes a report reflecting on the way in which the group went about the task given to it, how well it achieved its objectives and what has been learnt from the experience (20 per cent).

During the main project students produce a formal statement of requirements, a project plan and at least two progress reports. They also write two process reports in which they reflect on some part of their experience. These documents are read and commented on by tutors, frequently in great detail, and, on occasion, they are referred back for revision before being accepted. Their function is entirely formative. It is part of the philosophy of the course that students should be judged upon the level of competence which they demonstrate at the end of the course and should not be penalized for mistakes made along the way if these have been turned into opportunities for learning.

At the end of the course each student writes a dissertation which must contain a description of the main project in sufficient detail to enable the learning context to be understood. In addition the student must demonstrate his or her competence in project management by including evidence of the attainment of each of the course objectives and a commentary on the learning which had taken place during the course. The dissertation is submitted for assessment (70 per cent) and a presentation is made in the presence of the examiners.

REVIEW OF THE COURSE

Evidence for the success of the course can be provided in a number of ways. Over a period of nearly ten years it has grown from an intake of ten students a year to two cohorts annually with up to 20 students in each. This growth has continued during the economic recession of the last few years and many companies have placed students on the course over a period of time. The median age of the students has risen from 30 to nearer 40 and many of those who have taken the course recently already have substantial project management experience. A similar trend is observable in the scale and cash value of the main projects being undertaken. The benefits to the students are no less real, though harder to measure. A common observation by the course tutors is that many of the students show merely adequate performance until a point which is, perhaps, two-thirds of the way through the course when a dramatic improvement is observed. The effect is not unlike that of an aircraft taking off from the ground. This improvement in performance has, from time to time, been rewarded by employers by promotion before the end of the course. A number of the graduates from the course have been successful in introducing improved management methods in their companies. The conclusion can reasonably be drawn that the educational approach adopted has been very successful in achieving the aims and objectives of the course. It is therefore useful to review that approach in the light of current knowledge about experiential learning.

EXPERIENTIAL LEARNING

The world of experiential learning has been described in terms of four 'villages', each of which has its own aims and values (Weil and McGill, 1989). These villages are:

1.   The assessment and accreditation of 'prior' experiential learning.

2.   Experiential learning and change in higher and continuing education.

3.   Experiential learning and social change.

4.   Personal growth and development.

The course which is the subject of this chapter apparently lies firmly in the second village. But it also shares the objectives of the fourth village and the methods of the first village are employed in the assessment of the students. While, at first sight, there is less common ground with the third village, it may be observed that some of our graduates, individually or in groups, have been successful in challenging the established cultures of their companies and in becoming catalysts for change. The course is, therefore, distinguished by the breadth of its vision of the possibilities of experiential learning.

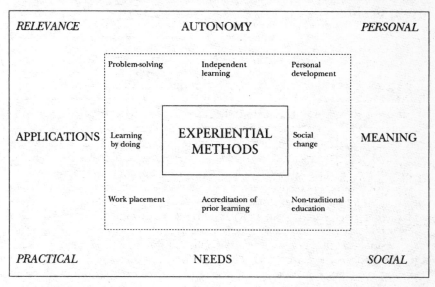

Figure 7.1 *Driving forces, foci and methods in experiential learning*

It is also useful to set the course in the framework of purposes and methods in experiential learning described by Henry (1989), adapted and summarized in Figure 7.1. The box bordered by the dotted line contains the main categories of learning experience. The outer box summarizes the driving forces in CAPITALS and the focus of learning in *ITALICS*. The driving forces are polarized on a horizontal axis (real-world applications vs meaning) and a vertical axis (student's own needs vs the needs of the environment). The words describing the focus of learning are each associated with a quadrant of the diagram. The learning experiences in the inner box are arranged to be appropriate to the driving force and focus of learning which lie closest to them. The course described in this chapter can be mapped readily onto the top half of Table 7.2. Virtually all the methods of experiential learning listed by Henry in connection with this area are employed somewhere in the course. The diversity of learning experiences and their appropriateness to the course objectives are evidently one of the reasons for its success.

Table 7.2 *Barriers to experiential learning*

	Fear	Inertia	Ignorance	Arrogance	Low self-esteem
Internalization and generalization	I'm afraid of the implications of it	I'm more comfortable as I am	I don't know how to think about it	I know it isn't worth thinking about it	It wasn't really any good
Testing	I'm afraid to try it	It's too much bother to try it	I don't know how to try it	I know it isn't worth trying it	Someone like me couldn't do that

During the first module the students are introduced to the theory of experiential learning as described by Lewin and others (Kolb, 1984). According to this theory the process of experiential learning takes the form of a cycle in which experience is internalized through reflection and generalized in the form of theories which can be tested, leading, in turn, to further experience. This is sometimes expressed more succinctly as 'do-learn-do'. The purpose of particular elements of the course, especially the set groups and the use of process diaries and reports, is explained in terms of their value in facilitating experiential learning. The process can be made more understandable to students whose previous education has been in the hard sciences if it is pointed out that the distinction between the words 'experimental' and 'experiential' is quite recent. What we now call experiential learning is gained by the application of experimental methods in the laboratory of everyday life. Through the operation of the experiential learning cycle an individual gains, over a period of time, a unique personal knowledge of the world which governs his or her habitual patterns of behaviour. In order to promote personal development it is necessary to ensure that the experiential learning cycle proceeds without impediment. But everyday experience provides abundant examples of ways in which people persist with unsatisfactory behaviour patterns in the face of evidence from experience that they should be abandoned or modified. It seems to us that the reasons for this can be summarized as fear, inertia, ignorance, arrogance and low self-esteem. These factors act as barriers to experiential learning at all phases of the learning cycle, as shown in the examples in Table 7.2.

Occasionally the barriers are swept aside by powerful external forces. But external pressure and encouragement, however well-meant, usually only serve to increase the barriers so that behaviour becomes even more defensive and no learning takes place. Thus in order to facilitate experiential learning it is important to remove the barriers rather than to find sticks and carrots with which to urge the students over them. Each student must find his or her own way of recognizing and dismantling the barriers if real learning is to take place.

The process of experiential learning can be supported in three ways: by mentors, by peers and by self-help. Each of these has its problems. The mentor (parent, teacher, coach), superior in knowledge and experience, is frighteningly competent and it can be very hard to admit one's underlying fears to such a person. The peer is believed to share one's own weaknesses and may provide valuable encouragement, but may also share prejudices and ignorance. Self-help (often in the form of a diary) can be very valuable but requires great self-discipline and does not provide an objective, external, viewpoint. The approach employed with success in the engineering project management course is, in effect, a combination of the three methods.

The set group combats fear with encouragement; arrogance and inertia with criticism; ignorance with ideas; and low-self esteem with peer group esteem. It has a fixed membership and becomes a learning team whose members are committed to each other's success. The stress placed upon the group by the linking project drives it rapidly through Tuckman's (1965) stages of forming, storming and norming so that it becomes an effective, performing, team. The development of a close-knit group enables the learning process to be undertaken effectively in an environment of trust. The set group advisers act as facilitators to the group, controlling its development with the objective of reaching the performing stage shortly before the sixth module. They also act as mentors to the group and its members and provide an external view of its operation. Although groups which operate without advisers have been effective (McGill *et al.*, 1976), our experience is that the advisers are sometimes needed to defuse conflict, to point a way forward to a group which has lost its way and to challenge a group which has become too cosy. We believe that the advisers, though present, should not be regarded as part of the group and we generally arrange the room to make that point clear.

The process diary offers a way of dealing with issues which are so sensitive that they cannot be revealed to anyone else. This combination of methods builds on the strength of each while providing antidotes to its weaknesses. We believe that this method of dismantling the barriers to learning is the key factor in the success of the course.

CONCLUSION

The experience of the Lancaster MSc in engineering project management has shown the great power for learning and personal development which can be unlocked when clearly specified and appropriate objectives are matched with a wide range of learning experiences in an environment which expects the students to be responsible for their own learning and which provides strong support for the processes of experiential learning. We believe that there could be great benefits in the application of this approach in other areas. This approach is not more onerous than conventional methods because the time and effort required to support the students' learning are saved from those normally required for teaching. It is, however, very important that the tutors should be trained in the skills needed.

Chapter 8

Information technology and flexible learning

Karen Valley, Chris Steeples and Patrick Hynes

INTRODUCTION

The main objective of this chapter is to provide an overview of how different types of technology can support independent learning.

The chapter begins by outlining three main categories of technology that can be used in teaching and learning. It then discusses ways in which the technology described offers support for independent flexible learning. Following this we present a successful model of independent learning supported by technology in the form of computer-mediated communications (CMC). The chapter ends with some conclusions about how information technology can be used to encourage and support autonomy and independence in learners. We also provide an assessment of future developments in technology-supported learning.

THE AVAILABLE TECHNOLOGY

The most widely used technologies in education currently are dedicated teaching and learning software (collectively known as courseware); computer-mediated communications technology; and networks providing global access to on-line resources and services (see also Chapter 9). Of these, only courseware can be regarded as a dedicated technology, specifically designed for educational use: communications technology and networks are used for many different purposes, of which education is one. As technology develops, such distinctions are becoming more blurred. We return to this point below.

Courseware

The term 'courseware' is used to describe software specifically designed for educational use: software that teaches users about a particular subject. A piece of courseware should have clear learning objectives and will ideally engage the learner in a number of interactive activities, although the amount of interactivity offered can vary (Laurillard, 1993). Types of courseware commonly in use in HE include tutorials, drill programs and simulations (Alessi and Trollip, 1991).

Tutorial programs typically present users with the subject matter to be learned, question them about it, and provide feedback on their responses. Feedback often takes the form of remediation of an incorrect response. The subject matter can be wholly procedural or conceptual, or a combination of both. Tutorials rarely allow users to practise a skill or to apply the presented information.

The main function of a drill is to provide practice, for example in applying a concept or in performing a skill. Drills have the same basic format as tutorials: after an introduction, an item is presented, the learner is questioned, and the system deals with their response appropriately. The number of repetitions of the present-question-respond cycle is determined by several factors. 'Drill and practice' is often criticized for making poor use of the power and flexibility of a computer: it is argued that more traditional media such as textbooks are equally good for this sort of task. Although drills are often over-used in courseware, good drills can have an important place in the set of tools available for technology-supported learning.

Simulations provide the opportunity to interact with some (often simplified) aspect of the world using a computer. The main difference between a simulation and a tutorial is that simulations allow users to interact directly with the simulated system by performing activities, solving problems, manipulating characteristics and so on. One of the main advantages of simulations is that users can interact safely with systems to which they may not have access in 'real life', for example because they are dangerous (such as nuclear power stations) or inaccessible (such as high gravity). Simulations can combine the functions of tutorials and drills, in that they can introduce the topic to be taught, present it, question users about it and respond to their answers, and provide practice sessions on it.

There is now increasing use of other software for learning, where the software itself does no actual teaching. Examples include data sets, used by students in subjects such as psychology and economics, or spreadsheet templates, used in subjects such as accountancy. Such software provides learners with runnable models and 'ideal' sample populations that they can manipulate. It allows learners to test hypotheses and engage in 'what-if' manipulations. However, it usually provides little guidance, support, assessment or remediation.

The simplest way for institutions to acquire courseware is to buy it off the shelf. This is a quick, easy and relatively cheap solution. In HE, courseware can be obtained from one of the many subject-specific Computers in Teaching Initiative (CTI) centres (see for example CTI, 1995). Additionally, the Teaching and Learning Technology Programme funded several courseware development projects in a range of subjects (TLTP, 1993; TLTP II, 1993). Two other options for courseware acquisition are to contract-out development to a specialist company, or to develop it in-house. Each solutions has advantages and disadvantages.

Computer-mediated Communications (CMC)

Non-dedicated technologies include systems that facilitate communication between individuals using networked computers. Collectively, such systems are termed 'Computer-mediated Communications' (CMC). We can distinguish between *synchronous* and *asynchronous* CMC systems.

Synchronous tools allow simultaneous connectivity between people who are physically separated. They offer flexibility in terms of place, but as with traditional teaching methods learners must be in a particular location at a particular time, using the appropriate equipment to be able to connect. Tools allowing synchronous working include videoconferencing, audiographics and desktop videoconferencing, and shared workspaces.

Where videoconferencing is used in HE, its main function is to deliver the type of large-scale, one-to-many lectures that have been the mainstay of university teaching over many years. Such mass lectures are extremely cheap to administer, allowing the servicing and throughput of large numbers of students. Videoconferencing technology allows the one and the many to be in different locations: groups of students at multiple sites can connect to a lecturer located elsewhere. Learners can see and hear a lecture via visual and auditory display screens and can ask questions. Lecturers can see and hear the different groups of learners and can respond to individuals directly.

The technology required to link sites is extremely specialist and may require considerable effort to set up and support. In addition to being complex and expensive, such tools are primarily facilitating transmissive forms of education that have long been considered pedagogically ineffective (Laurillard, 1993). Such systems provide little in the way of flexibility and interactivity for independent learners.

Desktop conferencing and audiographics are also synchronous tools. They support interaction and small-group working, often featuring a shared workspace that each person can see, control, manipulate and edit. Small windows allow the group to see who is talking. Such systems have been used to support distance learning in remote sites, for example, where learners are located at some distance from the tutor. This technology can emulate one-to-one teaching situations and one-to-small-group tutorial seminars. However, the tools are only effective and workable for small groups and are therefore not scaleable. As with other synchronous tools, they require learners and tutors to work at the same time, and again require access to the necessary equipment and technical support. Currently, desktop conferencing systems are extremely expensive and video links are not always reliable or completely synchronized, leading to frustrating or disorienting connections.

Asynchronous computer-mediated communications tools and systems are very different. Learners need not work simultaneously and have some degree of flexibility in terms of their learning location. Messages can be created and sent at one time and read at another. As participants are not connected at the same time, any contribution to a discussion has to be made in a permanent way, for example through a textual message. This permanence allows conversations to remain, for each participant to reflect upon, to reuse and to revisit. The largely textual nature of the communication encourages concise, considered and coherent contributions, and promotes the refinement of understanding and the development of writing skills.

Asynchronous CMC includes e-mail, on-line bulletin boards, computer conferencing systems and networked communal discussion databases (often termed 'groupware' or 'knowledge construction' environments). The common feature of these systems is that communications are prepared, edited, stored, received and sent using a computer or several computers connected in a network.

With e-mail the underlying metaphor is of one-to-one or one-to-group communication, amongst people who may be at different geographic locations. In sending or receiving an e-mail message, there is an underlying assumption about who will receive that message. The communication is essentially to named individuals.

With computer conferencing or bulletin boards systems, the underlying metaphor is of mainly textual communication into a 'public' space that all participants sharing a common interest may access. The database of texts is usually stored on a single computer, to which each user must log in. There is a sense of communicating to the topic, rather than addressing a message to named individuals. Conferencing tools and bulletin boards provide additional functionality over e-mail tools, enabling group processes such as a topic hierarchy structure, a voting mechanism for group decision-making, and searching tools to aid quick identification of information.

Networked communal discussion databases provide the ability to incorporate more than just textual messages. Conference discussions can contain video and audio clips, animation and graphics and we can switch seamlessly between different types of application – from word-processor, to spreadsheet, to conferencing discussion space. Thus, the interpenetration of e-mail, conferencing and communal databases is increasing.

A complete and coherent environment to support group working, learning and communication is developing on our desktops. Within this environment users can integrate and draw information from all areas of their on-line workspace, in a variety of formats and media types.

THE WORLD WIDE WEB

Computer networks can have a number of levels: a network in one room, a network at a particular site, the universities' network (JANET), and beyond. A global 'Internet' of connected computer networks has origins which go back 25 years. The Internet established a common standard, making it possible for all computers to communicate, regardless of platform (Macintosh, Windows, UNIX and so on). It also established a network of computers using a variety of communications technology: cables, telephone lines, satellite, microwave and so on.

Initially the power of the Internet remained largely confined to a relatively small set of researchers. With the arrival of the World Wide Web (The Web, WWW or W^3), many more have become aware of it. Previously, the Internet was used for predominantly text-based e-mail (see above). The Web brought graphics, sound and video, and more importantly, a user-friendly graphical interface. It is now relatively easy to search for, link to, and transfer information anywhere in the world. The essential concept of the Web is hypermedia: the ability to *click* on highlighted text or images, in order to move to another document, possibly on another computer in a different country.

There are estimated to be over 5 million computers permanently attached to the Internet, and at least as many systems again that are only intermittently on-line. The World Wide Web has emerged as a common standard for a public domain distributed hypermedia system, and is widely accepted as a prototype for the much talked about Information Super Highway of the future. As a relatively new technology it is only just beginning to find a place within education. For a detailed discussion of the Web's use in HE see Sangster (1995) and the Web-based Internet course, 'Internet for Everyone' (Internet for Everyone, http://www.mailbase.ac.uk:8080/ife/).

TECHNOLOGY AND INDEPENDENT LEARNING

Overall, the most obvious support for independent learning arises from technology that provides learners with flexibility of place and of time. For example, with courseware learners have subject matter and teaching expertise available whenever and wherever they need it. With asynchronous communications technology and network technology, learners can participate from anywhere with a connection, at any time.

An important effect of this is that access to education can be provided for people who may otherwise be excluded. This includes disabled learners; those with socio-economic constraints or caring responsibilities; adult learners who wish to assume more control over their own learning; and more passive and apprehensive learners, particularly those whose first language is not English.

We next discuss more specific ways in which the three types of technology described above can be used to support independent learning.

COURSEWARE AND INDEPENDENT LEARNING

Courseware provides learners with a means of learning that is independent of timetabled classes. They can run the system in their own time, either on their own computer or in a campus computer lab.

The ways in which courseware can be used depend very much on its content and type. Learning situations that could be supported by appropriate courseware include: review and practice of topics; exam revision; catching-up on missed classes; coverage of additional, possibly more advanced topics than is possible within the normal timetable; and practical work, particularly where it illustrates dangerous or 'invisible' concepts such as nuclear explosions or gravity.

It would be unrealistic to expect courseware completely to replace normal teaching activities. However, used appropriately, it can be an important and useful addition.

CMC AND INDEPENDENT LEARNING

We have aggregated a set of educational purposes for using asynchronous CMC systems, grouping them around a set of five 'models' for participation. These can be applied in many different subject areas.

Question and answer

Much of the learning in higher education is problem-based, often requiring answers to specific, but common questions encountered by learners. A computer-based conference database is a useful means of collecting frequently asked questions and answers. Questions can be addressed to tutors and to peers and both questions and answers can be stored. The database therefore becomes a permanent record that current and future students can interrogate. Tutors can also see the real concerns that students have, often discovering fundamental misunderstandings or gaps that might otherwise be missed. Gaining insights into the issues and problems confronting students can enhance the performance and professional development of tutors (Steeples, 1995b).

Electronic seminars

Seminars are essential for encouraging learners to engage in deep and meaningful ways with a subject. They allow learners to make personal sense of what they are learning about – essential if their understanding is not to be disembodied and inert. In HE it is increasingly difficult to provide opportunities for face-to-face seminar groups. These problems are exacerbated for more marginalized members of the student population.

By means of CMC the seminar can be restored, with added advantages. Students can work at their own pace, and can log into the conference at a time and in a place that best suit their needs. All discussions are accessible to all members of the group, and each student is given equal opportunity to contribute. Students can reflect before responding, with time to seek out a reference, to consult a source or to prepare a coherent reply.

Electronic seminars promote active participation in the learning process and deep engagement with the subject matter (Goodyear, 1994). In addition, in electronic discourse there is a sense of personal involvement and ownership that encourages students to take active roles to ensure group success.

Computer-mediated collaborative learning

Much significant learning is facilitated by communal environments. Understanding arises from the often chance conversations, arguments and debates in which learners engage: there is a social construction of knowledge. The process of sharing operates at two levels. First, the articulation enables students to refine their own understanding of concepts and ideas, revealing misconceptions or issues. Second, the articulation allows students to compare other perspectives and experience against their own.

Collaborative learning also promotes the development of meta-level, more generally applicable skills in group communication and coordination: the skills for collaboration and team-working that are essential for effective cooperation and communication in work settings (Steeples, 1995a). With CMC, we have new flexible ways of supporting group-based learning. Flexible team or project groups can be effected that are not tied to the constraints of timetabled meetings or specific locations.

Global classrooms

CMC environments can allow international groups of learners to be formed. This provides the opportunity for students to assess their own perspectives on a problem, measured against potentially quite different cultural perspectives of students located elsewhere in the world. A current project at Lancaster aims to have international student teams investigate a common topic by finding resources and services on the Internet. The teams will critically appraise those resources in a CMC environment. The teams will be drawn from universities in the UK, Ireland and the USA.

CMC also makes it possible for subject experts from outside the host institution to join discussions, widening the sphere of expertise available. Even if experts can only participate for a short period of time, their contributions remain available as long as the conference exists.

Ongoing learning and research communities

This model stems from our work on the JITOL project (Goodyear and Steeples, 1993). JITOL (Just-in-time IT-based Open Learning) was concerned with using IT to support ongoing programmes of professional development. Much of the expertise in fields of professional activity is distributed in individual practices, and the knowledge tied into those practices. In these situations, co-learners become an essential part of each other's education (Steeples et al., 1995).

The model is centrally concerned with giving distributed practitioners within professional communities timely, cost-effective access to current information (including expertise, experience and knowledge). This is best enabled by building and sustaining a two-way relationship between a community of learners and the service provider, who can define together what is known and what needs to be known. This can be continually redefined as new working practices emerge.

The day-to-day communication and information gathering and sharing is most efficiently provided via asynchronous electronic communications: ideas, knowledge and practices can be shared and are open to debate and refinement.

THE WORLD WIDE WEB AND INDEPENDENT LEARNING

The Web can support independent learning in three primary ways: by widening the range and volume of resources available; by enabling resources to be found; and by enabling multimedia resources to be delivered to the learner's desktop.

The effects of the Web on learning are more subtle. Already the Internet is encouraging people to expect information to be freely available. Within this culture of the information-literate, a group of people will grow who are already motivated to seek out information and to take responsibility for their own learning. Projects such as Netskills (http://www.netskills.ac.uk/) are addressing the escalating dependency of staff and students on networked information. The project aims to provide a much-needed training programme which will help shift the HE community towards effective and widespread use of networked information resources.

We have identified six main ways in which the Web can support independent learning. These range from tried-and-tested robust technologies to newer research-based technologies.

An electronic library of resources

At its simplest, the Web can be seen as a general-purpose, enormously rich information environment. Information is available on everything and anything and in many formats. Examples include research papers, project reports, cvs, calls for funding, lecture notes, slides from presentations, software, radio broadcasts, audio clips, graphics, video and animation clips. Although not specifically intended for educational use, such information can be invaluable to the learner.

The size of the Internet and its reach into every aspect of life is both its success and its potential problem. There is too much information available; learners can find it hard to locate relevant resources; and access times can often be too long to allow effective working. The problem of access speeds is being addressed through better use of existing technology and through more sophisticated new technologies.

The issues of better organization and easier location of information are also being addressed. For example, reference databases are one way of organizing information. This is the solution adopted by the Yahoo (http://www.yahoo.com/) site, a public-domain Web site dedicated to helping users find information. Other examples specific to HE include the subject-based CTI sites (http://info.ox.ac.uk/cti/) and the Social Science Information Gateway (SOSIG) (http://sosig.esrc.bris.ac.uk/). At SOSIG, all the available resources are described, classified and entered into a searchable database.

New sites are emerging that encourage people to make relevant information available, and that will classify the available information to make it searchable. A good example is One World On Line (http://www.oneworld.org/), a gateway to charities and other organizations who are concerned with global justice, conflict, aid, trade, education, health and human rights. Relevant organizations know where to broadcast their information; others know where they can find information on these topics. Sites such as this require a significant amount of investment.

New technologies are also emerging which seek to support the structuring, maintaining and delivery of information through new technological initiatives. One good example is Hyper-G (http://hyperg.iicm.tugraz.ac.at:80/) (Maurer *et al.*, 1993), providing advanced navigational tools that help users to orient themselves and avoid becoming 'lost in hyperspace'.

Delivering learning materials

The Web provides a useful delivery platform for learning materials, such as lecture notes, which might otherwise be delivered by less technological means. This is already happening at many HE institutions: for example, the City University Business School site (http://www.city.ac.uk/~sf309/trtop.html) is used to store and manage documentation. Although this could be achieved by other means, using the Web allows students to learn about the Internet. A similar rationale is used to justify making lecture notes available on the Web, with the added benefit of allowing teaching to be integrated within a larger framework of resources. In addition, any multimedia resources used during lectures can remain accessible to learners afterwards (Nott *et al.*, 1995).

Delivering courseware

Courseware tutorials can be delivered via the Web. One good example is *The Interactive Frog* (http://curry.edschool.Virginia.EDU:80/~insttech/frog/) (Kinzie *et al.*, 1995). The courseware is designed as a preparation tool or substitute for laboratory dissection of a frog. The courseware provides a guided tutorial with pictures and video clips. The student can choose to visit the parts of the tutorial which are of most use. However, currently the Web offers only limited interactive facilities.

A key feature of this type of Web use is that the courseware is run on the system where it is located, not on the user's own computer. This allows it to be run without concern for the type or configuration of the user's machine, and benefits learners using a computer with limited or protected disk space. A final advantage is that learners always access the most recent version of the courseware.

Interactive courseware

Interactivity is an important attribute of independent learning. Often, a course attains flexibility by reducing the amount of face-to-face contact. The Internet has the potential to move the focus of learning from the 'sage on the stage' to the 'guide on the side', while maintaining a degree of interaction. As the Web becomes more interactive, so it will provide further support for independent learning. We can already see some examples of this:

1. Interactive simulation models present users with a set of questions to complete. Their answers are automatically fed into a simulation model, and a response returned. For example 'Be your own chancellor' (http://www2.ifs.org.uk/) allows users to set a budget for the UK and to see its effects.

2. On-line assessment through systems such as MedWeb (http://medweb.bham.ac.uk/http/caa/caa.html). This uses forms to provide immediate feedback to a set of multiple-choice questions, with the option of tutorial support.

3. Interactive learning systems such as SuperCAL (http://www.staffs.ac.uk/supercal/supercal.htm), which makes use of software ToolBook™ to provide interactive elements to a Web tutorial.

4. New developments such as Java™ applets (http://java.sun.com/applets/applets.html). These allow interactive elements to be included within a Web page without the need for other applications. This ensures that the student needs no additional software or a particular computer configuration.

Combined with asynchronous conferencing

Interactivity can also be achieved through combining conferencing technology with the Web. The Lancaster project described above involves international teams of undergraduates investigating a common problem by identifying Web resources. They will then collaborate in their appraisal of those resources, using asynchronous CMC for support and discussion.

Systems that support both asynchronous conferencing and Internet use in a single integrated environment will soon be widely available.

Combined with real-time conferencing and virtual reality

Virtual reality (VR) enhanced networked learning environments are beginning to appear. One example, BIOMOO (http://bioinformatics.weizmann. ac.il/BioMOO/), combines a VR Web environment with real-time conferencing. This enables learners to interact within a virtual world that is responsive to their actions. Although this technology is still at the research phase, its potential is as great as the impact of multimedia on networked learning.

A MODEL OF TECHNOLOGY-SUPPORTED INDEPENDENT LEARNING

In this section we outline a successful model of independent, flexible learning that utilizes information technology to provide tutorial support and to facilitate learner collaboration. This is a hybrid model of distance learning that promotes exchange of experience and knowledge, designed around flexible learner-centred study patterns and activities.

The Advanced Learning Technology (ALT) programme was one of the first distance learning courses to be based around computer conferencing (Goodyear, 1994; Nicholson, 1994). The part-time programme is designed to support the acquisition and extension of the skills needed for the design, development, evaluation and use of advanced learning technology. It is open to anyone with an interest in ALT, and participants generally work in traditional training environments or in higher, further or adult education.

There are 12 self-contained modules in the programme. These can be taken independently or combined with other advanced work to gain a Diploma or an MSc in Information Technology and Learning. The modules cover both theoretical and practical aspects of ALT, and emphasize learning issues as well as technological concerns. Each module has a study pack containing a set of readings, audio-visual materials, example assessment tasks and a study guide giving the tutor's commentary on the materials. Every module has two 24-hour residential sessions, eight weeks apart. Between the two residentials, course members have a period of home- or work-based independent study, working with the pack of study materials. During this time, they can maintain contact with tutors and other course members through asynchronous CMC.

The conferencing system used currently is Caucus, a UNIX-based system. However, the lack of a good user-interface makes it likely that this will be replaced in the near future (Lotus Notes and First Class are being considered). Participation in the conference requires access to a personal computer and modem.

Each module has its own conference space, divided into topics, and each topic typically has several postings. These vary a great deal in content and style: long, short, humorous, serious, trivial and argumentative input can all be found. Participants can log on to the conference from anywhere at any time. Once there, they can read and post comments on the existing topics, or can start their own topic of discussion.

. Although the main participants in the conference are tutors and course members, invited guests are also welcome. The conference for one module had contributions from courseware developers in Germany, Italy and the USA. Another had guests from several universities in the UK, Canada, The Netherlands and the USA. This included authors of assigned readings, IT specialists with an interest in open learning, and students doing a similar course in an American university.

The use of conferencing removes the sense of isolation that distance learners can often feel. It provides a supportive environment where learners can communicate with tutors and, most importantly, can exchange knowledge and experience with one another. They can discuss issues raised by the course material, receive feedback from others on proposed assignment tasks, input ideas for residential sessions – in fact, anything that members of a more traditional course would discuss face-to-face. Moreover, they can do this from home or from work, at times which most suit them. Participation in the ALT programme must often be fitted around the demands of full-time employment, family life, and other commitments. The modular structure and flexible approach of the programme, combined with the normal facets of distance learning, help ease the burden of conflicting demands. This model of learning has the potential to provide access to training and education for a much broader range of people than more traditional approaches, without necessitating the disruption of important family and social networks. The use of learning technology in the form of computer conferencing further enriches the experience, removing the geographical boundaries and constraints of time and place often imposed on those seeking professional and personal development.

SUMMARY AND CONCLUSIONS

In this chapter we have tried to show how three main types of technology can be utilized to provide support for independent learning. The technology described has appeal to all areas of teaching and learning in HE, is relatively easy to adopt and implement and is widely available and affordable.

The chapter also described a successful model of independent learning supported by technology. Although designed as a part-time distance course geared for professional development, the model is generalizable to other areas of the curriculum, and is adaptable to flexible on-campus programmes.

We discussed courseware, asynchronous CMC and the World Wide Web as three separate technologies. However, it is already clear that the boundaries between them are fast disappearing. Tools and techniques specifically designed for educational use are being developed for general-purpose technologies. Integrated systems supporting all three technologies in one seamless environment are appearing. This suggests that technological developments will bring even greater support for more flexible patterns of learning in higher education.

Increasing technological awareness in learners, coupled with more powerful, affordable technology will bring many changes. An obvious practical benefit will be easier access to technology for all learners, for example with on-line access in student rooms. Increasing skills and provision will mean that technology can be used without discrimination, exclusion or marginalization of classes of learners. We can take advantage of this flexibility, encouraging reflection in learners, and the development of critical skills. More individualized programmes of study can be created, linking learners to cognate programmes anywhere in the world.

The main conclusion that can be drawn is that, used appropriately, technology has much to offer independent learners. It offers opportunities for diversity, and enables individual freedom of choice – crucial factors with increases in student mobility and diversification of the student population. However, technology is not a universal panacea. Computers are simply one more educational tool, and must be set up and used appropriately. Technology must be tied to particular learning needs and used in a relevant context: its use should be learner-led, not technology-led.

As educators we have a responsibility to ensure that educationally effective uses for the technology in teaching and learning are determined. Technology use with pedagogical purpose is required: we must not abdicate pedagogical responsibility to machines.

Chapter 9

Computers for teaching and learning

Gordon Doughty

INTRODUCTION

Does training students in the effective use of technology support independent learning? Can this lead to study taking place with greatly reduced input from teaching staff? This chapter identifies ways in which computers can best help teaching and learning in higher education and describes some ways of demonstrating the validity and usefulness of these tools and techniques. Particular attention is given to identifying the perceived needs of teachers and institutions in higher education and to shaping the technology to fit those requirements.

Apart from literature on the use of computers in education, this chapter is based on results emerging from the Teaching with Independent Learning Technologies (TILT) Project – one of the institutional projects in the UK's Teaching and Learning Technology Programme. TILT employs 13 contract staff who support 60 permanent staff and more than 2,000 students in 20 departments. The project is showing how information technology (IT) may be used to support more independent learning by students throughout a university. The project workers perceive all of the players as learners, and are concerned with how the institution can learn what matters and what to do.

HOW CAN COMPUTERS HELP TEACHING AND LEARNING?

IT enables an institution to *support* learning as much as to *deliver* learning (Committee of Scottish University Principals, 1992). Where such use can provide resources for learning that are more effective, richer, available for extended hours, and open to a wider range of entrants to higher education, computers will replace some lectures, laboratories and tutorials. Students will have greater control over timing and pace, and there will be more likelihood of resources suiting the style and stage of each student's learning. Of equal importance, teachers can expect to gain time for giving more individual attention to students, to be able to devote more effort to some

87

other aspects of the teaching and learning process, or to be able to make space for research or administration.

Curricula need to change to adopt the best teaching methods, including the use of computers if appropriate. Teaching resources must be modified. Properly integrated into the curriculum, IT can help with specific learning problems. In certain situations it can probably be more effective than any other media, for example in dynamic graph drawing; in creating models that are under student control; in running simulations to save equipment; by furthering drill and practice; through replacing material often covered poorly in crowded tutorials; or by providing illustrations for a lecture to improve visual communication. This certainly has been the experience of teachers in TILT in dentistry, engineering maths, statistics, zoology, languages, music and history.

Some of the benefits claimed to arise from the adoption of IT for teaching and learning are:

Benefits to students:

- better understanding
- greater access to information
- more control
- better feedback
- mistakes are made in private
- it can be more flexible and sensitive
- more enjoyable
- faster
- availability of extra learning resources
- greater choice of learning styles
- more individual attention
- more patient, non-judgemental testing
- more drill and practice
- students are able to work at own pace
- better communications through electronic media.

Benefits to academics:

- save time, in the longer term, on teaching, marking and administering
- more time for individual attention to students

- more flexible timetabling
- more time may be available for research
- better quality assessment ratings are possible.

Benefits to institutions:
- more cost-effective teaching
- better teaching quality assessment ratings may be attained
- creates a progressive image with students and funders.

IT can support learning in many ways. For example,

- by being a guide or aid
- through discovery learning
- through games
- through modelling
- through simulation
- through drill and practice
- by displaying animations of dynamic systems
- by providing tutorial activities
- through interactive multimedia
- through visualization
- by acting as an electronic instructor
- by being a revision resource
- through problem-solving activities
- as a tool for formative and summative assessment.

EXAMPLES

Learning in subject areas
Experience has shown that most traditional library skills teaching is hampered by:

- getting access to students at the right time for them
- the weight of numbers which makes individual attention impossible

- the wide range of expertise – or lack of it – among students
- the teaching methods enforced by these difficulties which give little opportunity for feedback or evaluation and keep the students in a purely passive role.

Computer-assisted Learning (CAL) packages have the potential to overcome many of these drawbacks. Evaluation has shown that the use of IT not only raises learners' interest level but also increases confidence in the use of computers. This is of great importance, not least because of the increased use of electronic sources in the library (Creanor and Durndell, 1994; Creanor *et al.*, 1995).

Hispanic studies has noted that computer-based work led to students requesting (and obtaining) additional classes. This was not because they found the work more difficult, but because it was more enjoyable and offered, in their opinion, a more clearly focused set of learning objectives than those found in other types of class.

With lectures, students need to absorb material at a fixed rate, or to make good notes. CAL can be used to cover material at the student's optimum pace. Test results with a package on basic numeracy indicate that the material covered by the courseware is more accessible, and offers more opportunity for practice on a computer, than textbooks and lectures. Reports indicate that self-paced work appeals to students and there is evidence (through a logging facility) that a number are returning to use the software as a resource for independent learning and revision (Doughty *et al.*, 1995).

In dentistry, longitudinal studies have been carried out over several years on the use of computer-based learning resources within a practical laboratory course in periodontology. Student attitudes were positive, as measured by a questionnaire, by informal observation and through discussion with tutors, demonstrators and the software developer. Over a four-week period, students were asked to keep a diary noting how confident they were about attaining the learning objectives of the different laboratories. As they worked through the tutorial, practical and CAL exercises, the diaries showed a marked increase in confidence for each laboratory.

Working in student learning groups

When working with computers, students are required to (or choose to) work alone, or in groups. This may be dictated by the availability of equipment, timetables and opening hours, but it would be best were it to be dictated by the requirements of sound learning strategies. Staff and students need to be clear that some packages are best used alone, while others are far better used in groups. There is evidence that group working helps to overcome problems with the learning technology and lets students concentrate on the learning (Shlechter, 1991). Effective learning groups may consist of students of different age, ability and year groups, operating with combined objectives and in a mutually supportive fashion. For example, TILT teachers have timetabled a three-hour session for mathematics software use, combining the first and second year students of a course.

Computer-mediated communication for teaching and assessment

IT provides staff and students with several communication tools:

- e-mail and electronic file transfer
- gateway to information and data banks
- conferencing
- collaborative work.

The twentieth century music history class is large, made up of a mixture of second, third and fourth year students from different degree courses. Conducting seminars entirely via e-mail avoids timetabling clashes as both students and staff participate at a time which suits them and, as the seminar groups are small with five students in each, all students have ample opportunity to contribute. The perception of staff is that not only has the level of participation increased dramatically in comparison with traditional seminars, but also the quality of the contributions has markedly improved. The debates conducted over the network are just as lively, but with the added advantage that students have time to reflect on and research their contributions. Students, originally rather wary of the novelty of the system, are now giving very enthusiastic feedback and report that the e-mail seminar is working well. Initial results indicate that the other objectives, such as making better use of staff time, easing timetabling clashes, giving students transferable skills and encouraging them to make full use of the IT resources provided by the department have also been achieved (Duffy *et al.*, 1995).

Productivity improvements from students' training in IT skills

IT provides productivity tools, such as tools for:

- numerical processing (spreadsheets, statistical analysis packages)
- word-processing
- desktop publishing
- database analysis and management
- control of equipment and instruments and data capture
- programming
- graphic design
- presentations.

Improvements in productivity can result from students being trained to work with these tools more independently of teaching staff. Early learning of study skills, with or through IT, can make students more effective learners overall. TILT has been studying the use of IT by student teachers. They are trained early in their first year to use standard software for word-processing, page layout and communications and learn to use spreadsheet, database and graphics packages, mainly through the integrated package *ClarisWorks*, Internet software and *HyperCard*. The students transfer skills learned with these packages to using learning material produced by other packages. Often this occurs with a critical awareness of the merits or otherwise of the new package's interface and other functions (Doughty *et al.*, 1995).

Large classes, wider access and varied range of skills intake

CALMAT and *TopClass* maths packages were selected for first- and second-year students on the Bachelor of Technological Education degree course to bring students with a very wide range of incoming mathematical ability up to a common level of achievement. The student intake ranges from recent school-leavers to many mature learners. Moreover, students have studied a wide variety of maths courses, some recently, some many years ago, and their familiarity with the topics varies a great deal.

Radical changes in the Scottish Higher Music syllabus have meant that not all first-year students have experience in some of the basic skills they need for degree work in music. The necessity for a large first-year class adds to the difficulties in bringing them up to standard. An integrated musicianship package helps to fill the gap without calling on extra staff resources, and enables students to work at their own pace in areas where they need extra help.

Formative evaluation used to integrate computers into teaching

University teachers and administrators require convincing that it is worthwhile to invest in IT for their teaching. Many kinds of evidence are demanded, for example:

- claims by authorities in the field
- peer acceptance
- 'scientific' proof
- claims made about the utility of the resource
- widespread adoption by others
- match between claims about a resource and the teacher's ideology
- evidence from case studies
- the results of teachers' own experiential learning.

TILT has promoted the use of formative evaluation to help teachers to integrate IT into their teaching. Design of CAL materials cannot be considered separately from the learning situations, nor from the learning outcomes expected, and certainly not from the process by which the learning is achieved and assessed (Laurillard, 1993).

Learning depends strongly on factors other than the courseware: for instance if courseware is optional it will probably not be used, but on the other hand if students know that material will be examined, then not only will they learn it but they may turn to textbooks to supplement the software. These experiences are consistent with the theory of the teaching and learning process offered by Laurillard, which suggests that learning depends on a specific set of activities and that what matters is whether all activities are covered by the complete teaching and learning situation, and not by a single component of it such as a piece of IT courseware. For instance, whether students learn much from simulations seems to depend strongly on whether they become active in generating questions and running trials to answer these, as opposed to going passively through suggested examples. The moral is that it is necessary to consider CAL resources and activities within the total learning context.

On one trial where students worked singly, only one student was observed to become active in this sense of generating questions and running trials. In another where students worked in groups, as was traditional in that laboratory class, discussion seemed to be leading to a more fruitful learning experience. Another factor was the spontaneous behaviour of the teacher, who would engage students with questions at opportune moments, thus reducing the tendency to 'get through the worksheet' without any thought or reflection. Besides that example, packages in dentistry and electronics have now been evaluated in use with two student cohorts, and the evaluations have led to modifications not only to the packages but also to the way they are used. After incorporating new resources into their teaching, staff are able to discover how to revise these resources and also other aspects of the learning situation as a whole.

TILT uses a battery of evaluation methods and instruments. Each particular study is designed to suit the goals of the evaluation, the particular IT courseware to be studied, and the teaching and learning situation in which it is to be used. Both open-ended and fixed-response instruments are used: the former allow surprises about unanticipated issues to emerge, while the latter give systematic comparative studies of the issues which were anticipated.

A prototypical design might have:

- A pre-task questionnaire to discover aspects of what each student brings to the session – for example, prior experience or personal motivation.

- Confidence logs, completed after each kind of activity.

- A learning test (quiz) administered at the start of the session, at the end of the session, and after a delay of some weeks.

- Study of learners' subsequent exam performance on one or more relevant questions.

- Post-task questionnaire to elicit personal reactions to the experience.

- Interviews of a sample of students.

- Observation and/or video-taping of one or more individuals.

A preliminary report from the evaluators is then presented to the teacher. Interpretations of the findings are sought and discussed. A formal report is produced, written mainly by the evaluators, but including the teacher's interpretations and perhaps conclusions, together with recommendations for future integration of the CAL material within courses.

FITTING IT TO TEACHERS' PERCEPTIONS OF THEIR TEACHING

Teachers' difficulties in adopting IT centre on lack of time, lack of support staff, lack of information and lack of suitable materials (Hammond *et al.*, 1992). The following are among the more common responses:

- 'No time to listen to you'
- 'Over my dead body'
- 'It will never work'
- 'Yes... but'
- 'What's in it for me?'
- 'They won't let me'
- 'We need more computers'
- 'Help me to do it NOW'.

Where these difficulties are overcome, teachers begin to focus on using IT wisely. Different kinds of IT, or ways of using it, will suit different needs. The IT provider must accommodate the many views that HE teachers hold on what is important in the teaching and learning process. Many teachers, knowing the whole process to be so complex, decline to adopt an academic approach to pedagogy. Nevertheless, some teachers hold strong positions, informed by psychology (cognitive and behavioural), philosophy (meaning, knowledge), educational research, and developments in their subject areas (artificial intelligence, control, design). Various views become fashionable at times (for example, behaviourism, constructivism). The ways in which teachers may see IT fitting into their teaching depend on these views. A few examples are given here, in very crude terms, of how a point of view on teaching and learning leads to a particular kind of CAL.

Those who emphasize expert knowledge structures see learning as acquiring the knowledge of an expert in the subject, the knowledge of a professional or a researcher. The teacher provides a representation of the subject's knowledge structure (as trees of prerequisites in a logical development) and makes it accessible to the students. Such teachers may prefer a learning package to display this structure. Again, CAL designed with a behaviourist bias that emphasizes formative assessment feedback may not permit progress through the package until questions have been correctly answered. For discovery learning, teachers may prefer a package simply to be a resource collection. To the constructivist, meaning depends on experience, implying that the teacher and students should negotiate authentic, complex, real-world tasks of great variety. This may lead to the use of large, complex CAL packages of information and simulation, or real IT-based information, such as rich database-style resources, or the World Wide Web.

Perry (1988) distinguishes nine stages of learning maturity and points to the need to support students as they transform from being receivers of facts; through accepting that knowledge is incomplete; to taking responsibility for learning, by seeking experts, and by comparing alternatives. It is very difficult to construct learning packages to work equally well at all these stages. The teacher must consider intervening often in their use, or adapting them to make several versions.

ADAPTING IT TO FIT INSTITUTIONS' SELF-PERCEPTIONS

Universities are undergoing rapid change. Currently in the UK there is an annual decrease in real funding per student, and increased competition for students between a larger number of universities. Cost-effectiveness has become of greater importance. IT and CAL are moving from the 'start-up' phase to the 'productive' phase (Leiblum, 1992) and there are great hopes of them providing gains in cost-effectiveness (Committee of Scottish University Principals, 1992; TLTP, 1993).

It is useful to be aware that the debate on which kinds of IT are adopted and the processes by which this can occur are affected by the ways in which those in power perceive their institution (Dixon, 1992; Doughty *et al.*, 1995; Middlehurst, 1993). Even within a single institution, such as the University of Glasgow, there are many different perceptions of the ways in which such a large complex organization behaves. There are many roles in a university, with diverse perceptions, attitudes and objectives that will influence academics' reactions to proposed changes. The dedicated researcher, the technophile, the degree course leader, the departmental budget holder, the faculty dean, the property manager, etc – each member of the university has his or her own perception of the ways in which new learning technologies may permit more independent and flexible learning to take place. Each sees opportunities and threats to their ability to balance their many objectives and priorities. Decisions may be made by committees, and comments such as these may dominate the arguments:

- 'Cost-cutting to balance the budget is our main priority'
- 'We can't give up laboratory space for computers'
- 'We need to enhance our research reputation, not spend on teaching'.

Other comments which tend to be less prevalent are:

- 'Educational research should guide us'
- 'Information technology will solve our problems'.

The IT proponents must recognize the subjective and ambiguous perspectives of different groups within the institution and participate accordingly in the political processes.

Decisions on adopting new technologies on a large scale require long-term survival as the criterion, rather than short-term gain. The adoption of new technology follows a pattern. Early research identifies something which may be of future benefit but needs much investment (in capital, training, and changes in staff). Even before it is certain that the technology should eventually be adopted, some organizations (maybe those investing in the original research) begin to use it. All must decide the timing and pace of their investment. If it is too soon and large, the costs outweigh the short-term benefit, and can cause collapse. If too late and slow, competitors gain all the business, and again there is collapse. In between there is a difficult judgement. The best strategy may be to have a sparse but knowledgeable network of staff aware of the potential of the technology, using it in a small way, and ready to move fast in adopting it in a big way.

The pace of technological change makes this a difficult but fascinating process.

ACKNOWLEDGEMENTS

The author gratefully acknowledges the work of the TILT team in producing these reflections, and has quoted extensively from their text in other publications.

Chapter 10

Recent research on student learning and the learning environment

Noel Entwistle

INTRODUCTION

This chapter is intended to provide a background to discussions about independent study and flexible learning. It will report some of the thinking about student learning which is emerging from recent research at Edinburgh and will use that work to discuss the types of learning environment in higher education which are most likely to support high quality learning. To do this we shall need to consider, first, what counts as high quality learning and how best to recognize and describe it.

In recent discussions about improving teaching and learning in higher education, a number of different terms have been used to describe what type of student learning we should be encouraging. Two of the terms are the focus of this collection – *independent study* and *flexible learning* – but we also need to note another term – *active learning* – which has been used extensively in recent staff development materials. Let us look, briefly, at what these terms have come to mean, starting with flexible learning.

The term 'flexible learning' was popularized in Britain within the Technical and Vocational Education Initiative (TVEI) and led to the description of a flexible learning framework designed to encourage a general shift in teaching practice. Flexible learning involves a movement away from formal, whole-class didactic teaching towards individual self-management of learning through the provision, by the teacher, of structured resource materials, together with opportunities for the negotiation of tasks, self- and peer assessment, and collaborative group work, often on 'real-life' projects. The ideas emerging from this work have certainly led to imaginative innovations in teaching which appear to have been successful. However, the evidence on outcomes has not been wholly convincing to date.

The TVEI projects led to an accumulation of reports from teachers and students using these methods which indicate consistently positive attitudes towards the innovation, and a belief that relevant knowledge and skills are being developed (Driver *et al.*, 1990). However, evaluations have also pointed

97

out serious problems of ambiguity in the way flexible learning has been described. Teachers tend to use different methods in different ways within the same category of innovation (Black *et al.*, 1991) and, while commenting positively on the methods, a substantial proportion of teachers find them difficult to implement, given the current curriculum pressures existing in schools.

Such difficulties and ambiguities do not in any way detract from the *potential* merits of adopting teaching methods involving flexible learning, but they do draw attention to two problems in judging the value of innovations in teaching and learning. First, innovative procedures may be introduced by teachers who do not fully understand the principles of learning which underpin them, and so may implement them in ineffective ways. Second, the established institutional climate and curriculum has such a powerful, constraining effect that even well-designed innovations may be unable to make much impact, at least initially, on the overall quality of learning. This problem is just as severe, if not more so, within higher education.

The other two terms we need to consider are 'active learning' and 'independent study', and these overlap to some extent. 'Active learning' has been used in higher education to emphasize the importance of students coming to grips with the course material – engaging with it, rather than passively accepting the work as a component of course requirements (De Nicolo *et al.*, 1992). Active learning also involves students in taking more responsibility for their own learning – relinquishing dependence on the teacher as the main source of knowledge, as the judge and controller of progress, and as the dispenser of encouragement and criticism. Active learners seek out the information they need, judge their own progress, and are self-motivated.

These same characteristics are also developed through 'independent study'. Lancaster University and North East London Polytechnic were among the first British institutions to offer degree courses in which students could negotiate their own programmes of studies. Although the term 'independent study' is used to describe such special arrangements which allow students substantial control over both how and what they study, independent studying in a more restricted form has always been a crucial component of higher education (see also Chapter 3). But there is concern that an increasing proportion of students are coming into higher education badly prepared for the types of studying required in higher education (Vermunt, 1989). As part of the Enterprise in Higher Education Initiative (EHE) to encourage the development of transferable skills, there has been more emphasis placed on the direct teaching of study skills, and more particularly on the encouragement of self-regulated learning (Zimmerman, 1989). For graduates as they move into the world of work, the characteristics of active learning – seeking out the information needed, monitoring effectiveness in learning, and becoming self-motivated – are of crucial importance and so need to be promoted more directly within degree programmes (see also Chapter 2).

We shall come back to the settings which can help to promote self-regulated learning later, but first we need to consider the type of learning which we want the more innovative programmes of study to encourage. What types of learning are we trying to promote?

CONCEPTUAL UNDERSTANDING

The literature on the aims of higher education indicates that, besides the obvious aims of ensuring that students acquire a body of technical knowledge of subject-specific skills and procedures, students in all subject areas are expected to develop a way of thinking which has been variously described as 'critical thinking' (Entwistle and Percy, 1973), 'post-conventional thinking' (Ashby, 1973), or 'relativistic reasoning' (Perry, 1970). When lecturers in different subject areas use these terms, the meaning is to some extent similar, and to some extent importantly different. Each discipline collects and uses evidence in rather different ways, develops concepts along contrasting lines, and constructs arguments somewhat differently. These differences are very important, and yet the similarities are also worth considering. Lecturers in all areas of study seem to value the following attitudes and habits of mind:

- adopting a distinctive way of thinking about concepts, evidence, and theories

- taking a distanced, critical stance towards subject matter, assumptions and explanations

- tackling issues systematically, logically and effectively

- examining the adequacy of evidence and checking alternative interpretations

- demonstrating a thorough understanding of complex, abstract concepts within the discipline

- writing clearly and cogently, following appropriate academic styles and conventions

- being able to set and solve problems by applying concepts and techniques appropriately.

Underlying all these intellectual qualities is the idea that students should develop a thorough conceptual understanding of the subject area. The emphasis within the Enterprise in Higher Education initiative on additional 'transferable skills' which employers consider to be of great importance in graduates has been a necessary corrective to the overly academic stance of many traditional degree courses. It is sensible to see to what extent students can also be given opportunities to develop skills associated with, for example, realistically complex problem-solving, initiative and planning, collaborative work, and effective communication, both orally and in writing, designed for non-specialist audiences (Entwistle, 1992a). But these skills are necessarily 'additional', in that an effective professional must also have developed a thorough conceptual understanding of the academic discipline and the distinctive way of thinking which it demands. Only then can the 'transferable skills' be brought fully into play. That is not to devalue these skills, but to see their specific contribution to a graduate's intellectual armoury. They ensure that the technical knowledge acquired in degree courses can be used more effectively, and with less additional training, within the work place and they also offer specific skills which would not otherwise be in the graduate's repertoire.

What, then, is at the heart of academic learning in higher education? How do students set about reaching conceptual understanding for themselves? Here, we turn to research on student learning, and in particular to the research on contrasting approaches to learning.

CONTRASTING APPROACHES TO STUDYING

It may be helpful to remind you of the defining features of the two main approaches to learning, as identified by Ference Marton and others (see Table 10.1) (Entwistle and Marton, 1994; Entwistle and Ramsden, 1983; Marton and Saljo, 1984). In each approach, the main distinguishing feature is the intention – to understand ideas for yourself (deep), to cope with course requirements (surface), or to achieve the highest possible grades (strategic). These different intentions lead to contrasting study strategies and learning experiences.

In the deep approach, the student is essentially *transforming* the learning material in the process of making sense of it in relation to previous knowledge and experience, while a student adopting a surface approach is simply *reproducing* the material as accurately as possible. The main component of the strategic approach is *organizing* time and tasks, but always with a eye to what will produce high marks.

It is important to make it clear at this stage that an approach is not seen as a stable characteristic of the student. Approaches do vary, depending on the task demands, the assessment procedure, the reaction to the teacher, and on the learning environment as a whole. Yet students also seem to develop habits in studying which may lead them to rely more on one or other approach.

The most recent research we have been carrying out at Edinburgh has built on the idea of contrasting approaches to studying along three main lines:

- exploring the experience of academic understanding

- identifying and helping students at risk from ineffective study methods

- describing learning environments which support active learning and a deep approach.

Let us look at each of these in turn.

Table 10.1 *Defining features of approaches to learning*

Deep Approach   *Transforming*

Intention – to understand ideas for yourself

by

relating ideas to previous knowledge and experience;
looking for patterns and underlying principles;
checking evidence and relating it to conclusions;
examining logic and argument cautiously and critically;
becoming actively interested in the course content.

Surface Approach   *Reproducing*

Intention – to cope with course requirements

by

studying without reflecting on either purpose or strategy;
treating the course as unrelated bits of knowledge;
memorizing facts and procedures routinely;
finding difficulty in making sense of new ideas presented;
feeling undue pressure and worry about work.

Strategic Approach   *Organizing*

Intention – to achieve the highest possible grades

by

putting consistent effort into studying;
finding the right conditions and materials for studying;
managing time and effort effectively;
being alert to assesment requirements and criteria;
gearing work to the perceived preferences of lecturers.

The experience of academic understanding

We have seen that thorough conceptual understanding is at the heart of the traditional aims of higher education, and that it is also central to the deep approach to learning. Yet, are we really clear what conceptual understanding actually involves? It came as a shock, having worked with the concept of the deep approach for many years, to realize how little the term 'understanding' is itself really understood. The literature on cognitive psychology largely ignores the term, while educationists seem to assume its meaning is so widely accepted that definition is unnecessary. In practice, if you ask a group of experienced teachers to explain the meaning of 'understanding', they find it very difficult. If we want to suggest to colleagues how best to facilitate learning for conceptual understanding, we need to be clearer ourselves about what is involved.

In higher education, students are expected to learn how to think and use evidence in ways that are characteristic of the discipline they are studying. The essence of understanding is the connection between new ideas and what a person already knows. It is thus, necessarily, individually constructed. In developing effective conceptual understanding, students have to construct their own frameworks of interpretation from the evidence, arguments and explanations they have heard and read. The extent to which students will be able to construct fully independent frameworks will depend, to some extent, on the discipline. In the humanities and social sciences, these constructions can incorporate personal experience to a greater extent than in the sciences. But even in studying science, students necessarily come to understand concepts in somewhat idiosyncratic ways. They use the available representations of the abstractions in contrasting ways – some more visual and some more mathematical, for example.

Diana Laurillard has argued (1993) that academic learning has to be distinguished from everyday learning – it involves a difference between acquiring 'percepts' and 'precepts'. Much of academic learning is not just abstract, but it depends on thinking in 'approved' ways. Laurillard argues that the task of the teacher involves mediating learning. It is essentially a rhetorical activity in which the teacher seeks to persuade students to change their ways of making sense of various kinds of phenomena, using the concepts and ways of thinking characteristic of their discipline. The independent frameworks that students develop are thus constrained by the history of the discipline, and yet retain elements of individuality. To make this discussion more concrete, let us look at some recent research.

Two recent small-scale research studies in Edinburgh have been exploring the nature of understanding through probing the experience of students after completing their revision for finals and after writing coursework essays (Entwistle and Entwistle,1991). Here, results just from the work on revision will be introduced.

In planning this research it was felt that the experience of the lengthy period of revision leading up to finals, together with the demands of examinations themselves, would enable students to give first-hand accounts of what was involved in developing and using conceptual understanding.

Analysis of interviews showed, first, that there was broad agreement about what students had experienced. But subsequent analyses drew attention to marked differences among students in the forms of understanding they were actually seeking. Students repeatedly commented that the experience of understanding generally had a feeling tone associated with it – there was necessarily an emotional response, at least where significant understanding had been achieved. The inseparability of cognitive and emotional components of understanding was very clear in the comments made by the students.

Within our sample, as Table 10.2 shows, understanding was experienced as a feeling of satisfaction, although that feeling varied in its expression from the sudden 'aha', as confusion on a particular topic was replaced by insight, to a less dramatic feeling associated either with being able to follow a lecture or with an emerging appreciation of the nature of the discipline itself. This feeling was derived from a recognition of the meaning and significance of the material learned, and on occasions had its origins in previous personal or professional experience. Relevance and interest have often been shown to be closely associated with the deep approach to learning (see, for example, Entwistle and Ramsden, 1983).

The feeling of understanding also included a recognition of coherence and connectedness. The idea of 'things clicking into place' or 'locking into a pattern' was frequently mentioned, and this conveyed an implication of completeness. However, students often commented that their understanding might well develop further, and a category of 'provisional wholeness' was thus introduced. The students seemed to be experiencing 'closure' – feeling that the current understanding is satisfactory – and yet also anticipating from their previous experience that their current understanding might well be adapted and extended in the future. This almost paradoxical combination of completeness and potential for further development does seem to be an important facet of the concept of understanding. Associated with wholeness, there was also a recognition of the relative irreversibility of the understanding achieved – at least once it had been thoroughly established. Again, there seems to be an element of paradox in the idea of irreversibility combined with further development. Students appeared to be indicating that they expected the general pattern of interconnections to remain stable, while anticipating the possibility of further refinement, or the addition of more detail with which to fill out the pattern.

The feeling of coherence and connectedness led students to express confidence about explaining – a belief that they could provide a convincing explanation of what they had come to understand, either to themselves or to others. This confidence can be seen as another emotional component within understanding. It was often seen in the students' comments in a negative form – as anxiety, even panic, associated with feeling of being unable to explain something adequately for examination purposes. Students also said that understanding provided them with flexibility in adapting and applying ideas and information effectively. It was this confidence, both in being able to provide a convincing explanation and to adapt ideas flexibly for use in varying and novel contexts, which distinguished 'understanding' from 'knowledge' in the students' descriptions.

Table 10.2 *The experience of understanding during revision for finals*

General experiences of acquiring understanding:

- Feelings of satisfaction
- Meaning and significance
- Coherence, connectedness, and 'provisional wholeness'
- Irreversibility
- Confidence about explaining
- Flexibility in adapting and applying.

Contrasting forms of understanding being aimed at:

- Absorbing facts, details, and procedures related to exams without consideration of structure
- Accepting and using only the knowledge and logical structures provided in the lecture notes
- Relying mainly on notes to develop summary structures solely to control exam answers
- Developing structures from strategic reading to represent personal understanding, but also to control exam answers
- Developing structures from wide reading which relate personal understanding to the nature of the discipline.

To put the experience of understanding in the students' own words:

> it is the interconnection of lots of disparate things – I think that's probably the best way to describe it – the way it all hangs together, the feeling that you understand how the whole thing is connected up – you can make sense of it internally.... (When you don't understand) it's more just confusion, it's not clear cut. If I don't understand, it's just everything floating about and you can't quite get everything into place – like jigsaw pieces, you know, suddenly connect and you can see the whole picture.... But there is always the feeling you can add more and more and more.... (Really understanding), well, for me, it's when I could tell somebody else, if I was asked a question, and I could explain it so that I felt satisfied with the explanation... with a conclusion that is satisfactory to yourself as well as to others. (When you understand like that)... you can't not understand it (afterwards). You can't 'de-understand' it! (Composite taken from several students, from Entwistle and Entwistle, 1992)

In analysing the differences between students, it became clear that students were using the term 'understanding' in quite different ways. Their descriptions differed in terms of breadth (how much material was being brought together to create an understanding), depth (the variety and strength of the connections made within the material and to related ideas), and structure (the principles of organization used to provide a scaffolding for those connections). The forms represent a hierarchy (see Table 10.2), with the last category being what most staff would hope their students would aim for.

The study was not large enough to indicate what proportion of students would predominantly aim for which form of understanding, but there was a worrying suggestion that the second category (accepting and using only the knowledge and logical structures provided in the lecture notes) might prove the most common, and indeed that some exam questions might well require no more than that. This category implies that the student is accepting the lecturer's understanding without developing it into a personal framework that creates a deeper meaning, and leads to answers which 'parrot' lecturers' arguments and borrow their examples and evidence. The result is superficial knowledge mimicking conceptual understanding which may be difficult for an examiner to detect.

The first category – absorbing facts, details and procedures related to exams – was used, in the sample, only by medical students in referring to their experience in pre-clinical exams, which again was worrying. The only first-class degrees were awarded to students in the penultimate category (developing structures from strategic reading), who combined a deep approach with a strategic awareness of the demands of the examination system.

The final category described students who were predominantly concerned with their own conceptual understanding of the content, but as a result they seemed to lack an equivalently clear awareness of examination requirements. As one student said:

> Well, there were cases where I knew too much... I had to go through all the stages of working through (the topic) and showing that I had understood it. I couldn't gloss over the surface. And once I started writing, it all just 'welled up'. I felt that I couldn't interrupt the argument half-way, as it was developing... (because) it ties together as a whole. It's very difficult to pick something like that apart, when you understand the theory like that. Half an understanding doesn't make sense!
>
> *I:* Are you saying that you have to explain it in the way you understand it for yourself?
>
> Yes. It's essential to demonstrate your understanding of the whole, and its implications and limitations.... You could say I shouldn't be (doing) that in an exam, but basically I have to do it that way, because that's me. Anyway, gearing your learning too closely just to previous exam papers seems a bit like a form of cheating to me. (Entwistle and Entwistle, 1992)

Discussions of the transcripts with Ference Marton, triggered by one particular extract, led to a reanalysis of certain sections of the transcripts (Entwistle and Marton, 1994). The extract which suggested this particular reanalysis came from a student who was able to reflect particularly clearly on how she used her revision notes and brought them to mind on demand. Her general strategy in revising each topic involved 'concising' voluminous notes, step-by-step, down to a simple framework which she then used to rehearse her own understanding. Her experience of using these frameworks involved something like visualization, and yet not quite. She experienced her understanding in a quasi-sensory way, knew what was there, could 'see' the main points in her final summary notes, and was confident that more details were linked to the main points and could be retrieved when required.

The subsequent analysis of the whole set of interviews suggested that this experience was not uncommon, although the majority of students found more difficulty in articulating their experiences. Piecing together the range of incomplete descriptions, we concluded that students were experiencing their understandings as having some internal form and structure – almost as entities in their own right – and these came to control their thinking paths in some way (Entwistle and Marton, 1994). The term 'knowledge object' has been used to describe the essence of these quasi-sensory experiences of aspects of understanding. Focusing on key points within their knowledge object would 'pull up' additional information which they had memorized separately. In the words of another student, describing his ability to visualize a diagram he had been revising,

> I can see that virtually as a picture, and I can review it, and bring in more facts about each part…. Looking at a particular part of the diagram sort of triggers off other thoughts. I find schematics, in flow diagrams and the like, very useful because a schematic acts a bit like a syllabus; it tells you what you should know, without actually telling you what it is. I think the facts are stored separately… and the schematic is like an index, I suppose.

The knowledge object also seems to be used to provide flexible control of an examination answer as it develops. There is a dynamic interplay between the knowledge object and the demands of the question which creates essentially a unique answer, but the knowledge object seems to create a generic structure for a topic which is likely to remain consistent. Some students seem also to use the knowledge object to monitor the adequacy of their explanations, and in some comments it was even given an independent existence – at least metaphorically:

> Following that logic through, it pulls in pictures and facts as it needs them…. Each time I describe (a particular topic), it's likely to be different…. Well, you start with evolution, say… and suddenly you know where you're going next. Then, you might have a choice… to go in that direction or that direction… and follow it through various options it's offering…. Hopefully, you'll make the right choice, and so this goes to this, goes to

this – and you've explained it to the level you've got to. Then, it says 'Okay, you can go on to talk about further criticisms in the time you've got left'.

The term 'knowledge object' is used to describe an experience. It is *not* intended to suggest that knowledge is a commodity which can be transferred from teacher to student. Quite the opposite. The whole essence of the knowledge object is that it is a personal construction which provides a mnemonic structure to summarize complex interconnections that have developed in the process of developing conceptual understanding.

One of the strengths of this type of qualitative research which describes students' experiences of learning is that the results should describe a 'recognizable reality'. The idea of a knowledge object should tally with experiences of many students – at least those who have actively tried to construct meaning for themselves.

We are currently analysing interviews with students about coursework essays to see to what extent similarly tight bundles of knowledge are developed. Our preliminary conclusion is that the knowledge objects formed in essay writing are much less firmly established than through extensive revision and occur only when the students engage personally with the topic. In our sample, most of the students interviewed seemed to be far too strategic in their approaches to essay writing for this to occur. But, of course, many of the students revising for finals were being equally strategic, and relied heavily on reproducing the understandings of their lecturers. Only those students fully committed to a deep approach created clearly defined knowledge objects.

If we are to help students not only to be active in their learning, but to develop individual frameworks which help them to develop effective conceptual understanding, we shall need to examine teaching methods carefully to see how this way of thinking can be enhanced and supported.

Students at risk from ineffective studying

It may well be that the aim of thorough conceptual understanding goes beyond the intentions of a substantial proportion of students. And some students, particularly in the first year, encounter difficulties in studying which interfere even with basic comprehension, let alone conceptual understanding. They find difficulty in adjusting to the experience of higher education and adopt coping ploys in their studying that become increasingly ineffective as time goes on. Other recent research at Edinburgh has focused on trying to identify students who have particular kinds of study difficulty and of finding ways of helping them.

Inventory measures of approaches to studying have been criticized for implying that study strategies can be treated like fixed traits – that those approaches are consistent and difficult to change. The evidence suggests, in fact, that approaches to studying are relatively stable, although they are influenced by the experiences of a particular course of study. For example, Thomas (1986) showed that changing the method of assessment caused changes in the overall level of deep and surface approaches in a class. Changing from a multiple-choice test to an essay-type examination altered the students' inventory scores, lowering the surface scores and increasing the deep scores. But he found that the rank order of students within the class on the two approaches remained much the same. For some purposes at least, the use of inventory scores can be justified, as long as the scores are not considered totally accurate, wholly general, or immutable.

We have been using a modified and shortened version of our Approaches to Studying Inventory, which produces scores on deep, surface and strategic approaches to studying, to identify students at risk from ineffective study strategies. As part of the Teaching and Learning Technology Programme, we have developed three interacting computer programs using *HyperCard* on a Macintosh computer.

The first program is a questionnaire which collects background information, presents the revised inventory, and then asks questions about specific study skills, like taking notes and essay writing. The second program collects the data from a whole class of students, scores them, and presents a three-dimensional plot of the scores in ways which allow staff to identify students whose current study strategies and self-reported study skills seem to put them at risk. Our original idea was to leave departments to mount workshops and provide individual advice to help the students identified as having difficulty, but discussions with departments indicated that staff felt that they had neither the time nor the expertise to offer such help.

We therefore developed a third program which offers advice on study skills and strategies to students, and which can be used either in conjunction with the previous two programs or on its own. What we have tried to do is to use the opportunities offered by a hypertext environment to provide advice at different levels of detail and complexity, and encourage students to work their way through those levels in their own way. The advice itself draws on the student learning literature by putting repeated emphasis on students *reflecting* on their current ways of studying and considering alternatives – in other words on self-regulation. It also stresses the importance of recognizing the purpose of any study activity and of matching the study strategy to that purpose. The actual topics dealt with are those commonly found in study skills manuals, but the presentation and the emphasis is sufficiently different, hopefully to prove more effective than many current attempts to support study skills. Over the next year we shall be carrying out field trials to explore how the programs are used by departments and students, and how they react to them.

Learning environments for deep, active learning

We now come back to the question raised earlier. How can we arrange learning environments in higher education which will support deep, active learning and help students to develop conceptual understanding? This final section deals, not with actual research at Edinburgh, but draws on our attempts to analyse the effects on learning of different types of teaching (Entwistle, 1992b). Do the defining features of flexible learning and independent study suggest that they will support the types of learning which seem to be at the heart of higher education?

From what was said initially, flexible learning may involve:

- providing structured resource materials
- offering negotiation of tasks and topics
- encouraging self- and peer assessment
- devising 'real-life' projects for collaborative group work.

From the student's perspective, it will involve:

- taking more responsibility for their own learning
- relinquishing dependence on the teacher
- seeking out the information independently
- monitoring their own progress, and
- becoming self-motivated.

The value of collaborative learning was recognized by the students interviewed in Edinburgh. In commenting on developing understanding during the revision process, one student said:

> Quite often (I'd) ask a friend just to explain (something) – and they'd tell me 'Look, you're being stupid, you've missed this!'.... (At other times) we would sit down (as a group) in the library, or in the coffee bar, and just talk things over, and that helped. (To begin with) you think 'Oh, discussing it ! I'm going to feel really out of it.' But if you've done the work, and they've done the work, you actually learn it a lot better.... You've got to argue your case, because they have a different point of view to it, and that (process) worked fine. (Entwistle and Entwistle, 1992)

Students in the interviews lamented the fact that their discussion groups had been formed only at the very end of their higher education. Other students provide an excellent resource for testing provisional understanding and yet there are still few opportunities built into courses which allow this to happen.

There is accumulating evidence that any of the opportunities provided through flexible learning and independent study is likely to support the development of active learning. There is, however, less evidence that these approaches necessarily support the development of thorough conceptual understanding (Gibbs, 1992a). They *may*, and *some* do. But there is a real danger that the activities provided, and the stress on independence, can become divorced from the content and the types of thinking and learning which are being developed through them. Resource materials can be designed to encourage deep approaches, but they can equally make surface approaches much easier for students. Independent study can foster critical analysis or protect students from the need to demonstrate it. Collaborative project work can lead to in-depth discussions of conceptual problems, or passing a pleasant afternoon chatting.

In thinking about the advantages of flexible learning, or any innovative method, it is essential not to attribute outcomes to methods without qualification. That applies equally to traditional methods of teaching. There has been a tendency recently for some staff developers to denounce the use of lectures and traditional tutorials as always leading to passive learning. Yet there is plenty of evidence that *good* lecturing and tutorials can stimulate thinking during their subsequent individual work, and so help students towards high levels of conceptual understanding. Indeed, the students interviewed at Edinburgh had experienced only those traditional methods, and yet some of them had developed a very sophisticated understanding.

A good lecturer can evoke deep approaches (Hodgson, 1984) by presenting students with challenges through a critical, analytic attack on subject matter, and by encouraging them to explore ideas openly and imaginatively. Lecturers can also 'think aloud' so as to model the thinking processes characteristic of the discipline, with students being shown explicitly how evidence is used to reach conclusions and build up theories. This technique is particularly valuable in displaying explicitly to students the thought processes lecturers themselves use in developing understanding within their discipline and producing appropriate organizing principles.

A study currently nearing completion at Edinburgh is looking at how tutors encourage their students to develop conceptual understanding in conventional social science tutorials. What is particularly interesting is the way the best tutors seem to challenge the students to think critically, and yet at the same time encourage and support them in the difficult process of developing more complex conceptions of the discipline. They create a climate in which misunderstanding is accepted as a necessary step along the path towards understanding.

What we urgently need is a similar analysis of innovative methods of teaching to discover which particular ways of implementing them lead to deep outcomes of learning – and, of course, also what to avoid in using them. Moreover, there is a danger in believing that a method which works well for oneself, and for some students, will work equally well for colleagues, or for all students. The evidence on student learning is quite clear. Students differ markedly in the ways they prefer to learn, and react to teaching methods very differently (Pask, 1988). Yet reports on innovations are often presented in unqualified and over-enthusiastic terms, without making clear how dependent success will be on the context and the individuals concerned. I am reminded of a comment made by Friedlander (1975) in describing 'open', or progressive, elementary education in the USA:

> It is a gross oversight of available knowledge in psychology to assume that looser structure in the environment of the classroom is of some benefit for

all children, just because it is of great benefit for *some* children. It is predictable that children who have a low tolerance for ambiguity and uncertainty would find an open classroom which operates very successfully for some children, extremely threatening and anxiety provoking. It is also predictable that personality configurations of administrators and teachers who seek out the challenge of innovation in developing the open classroom would tend to be unmindful of the valid needs for order, predictability, and specificity for persons unlike themselves. (p.467)

Rather than castigating any method of teaching, or seeking to promote another, we need to find out a great deal more about the purposes for which different methods are best suited. Dahllof (1991) has recently commented:

Another limitation of current practice is that too much attention is directed towards finding or training 'the good teacher' and 'the best method', even though fifty years of educational research has not been able to support such generalizations. Instead we should ask which method – or which combination of methods – is best... for which goals, for which students, and under which conditions. (p.148)

My own view is that we need to explore the provision of a variety of methods of teaching designed to allow students to explore their own preferred ways of learning through guided choice and self-monitoring of their own reactions and progress. This seems to me to be at the heart of flexible learning, and the idea of independent study also requires the opportunity for relatively free choice among a variety of alternatives – including both innovative and traditional ways of learning. For both logistical and educational reasons, it seems best for degree courses to be planned in ways which provide maximum support and control in the first year, and an increasing requirement for flexible learning, independent studying and peer group work as the course progresses.

Even so, there is still a danger of becoming too idealistic. Higher education does involve certification of competence, and this can run counter to freedom of choice, at least in terms of content. From our own perspective, we may be too ready to associate innovation with quality. I have argued that innovation may or may not lead to higher quality learning. What evidence we have suggests that it all depends. It depends on the extent to which the innovation fits the objectives of the course, and also on the capabilities of the teacher or designer of the learning materials, and on the particular learners involved. It also depends, above all, on the messages that assessment convey – what types of learning are being rewarded. The single, strongest influence on learning is surely the assessment procedures and, as we saw in our interview study, even the form of the examination questions or essay topics set can affect how students study. Any mismatch between the teaching provided and the assessment demands creates difficulty for the students and may create resentment. Innovative teaching leading to conventional examinations can run into severe problems through such a mismatch.

It is also important to remember that entrenched attitudes which support traditional methods of teaching and assessment are difficult to change. It is not realistic to expect either sudden or dramatic changes. Attempts to move too quickly may lead to antagonism from colleagues. Rather, we need to work on a more evolutionary strategy that allows us to support examples of good traditional teaching, while offering more innovative alternatives. We need to take full account of the very real difficulties under which colleagues are currently being required to operate, with competing pressures between quality assessments of research and teaching and a progressive reduction in the unit of resource for teaching in many institutions.

In this situation change can only come about gradually. As Biggs (1992) has commented:

> If we are interested in redesigning learning contexts... (we need) to balance what is officially wanted, what is technically possible in the circumstances of that institution, and what has evolved so far through consensus amongst colleagues.... (Moreover), tradition, habit and convenience hinder enlightened change. The remedy, ultimately, can only be honest reflection on an institutional basis.... We need to change staff conceptions of teaching and learning, and to increase staff awareness of the relationship between teaching procedures, learning activities and learning outcomes. (pp.1, 23–4)

Chapter 11

Developing modes of independent study in a professional school

David Boud

How can a large school or department incorporate independent study and flexible learning into its activities? What strategies have been successful and what are the pitfalls to be avoided? What issues does this raise? While it is relatively straightforward for individual staff to adopt independent study approaches within the parts of the courses for which they are responsible, it is much more challenging to do this across entire courses and throughout an entire department.

The aim of this chapter is to focus on a particular school (comprising three departments) which has been successful in this process, to describe the main features of independent study which have been developed and to explore factors which have fostered the development.

BACKGROUND

The School of Adult and Language Education at the University of Technology, Sydney (UTS) has been the largest provider of award courses for adult educators in Australia. Courses were offered at all levels, from diploma through bachelors, postgraduate diplomas and masters to doctorates. Fields covered include adult basic education, teaching of English as a second or other language (TESOL), community adult education, Aboriginal adult education and human resource development. Since the first courses were offered for adult educators 15 years ago, this school (and its predecessors) has had a strong commitment to independent study and flexible modes of delivery.

While the entry requirements that students be of mature age and concurrently engaged in appropriate professional practice focused attention on the need to be responsive, the teaching philosophy of the school required that its courses be arranged to meet the needs of the students and the field of practice, as well as academic standards.

113

It was not a smooth path towards developing independent study, however. There was uncertainty in the early days about whether there would be sufficient students available to allow courses which followed this pattern to survive. Staff without a background in and familiarity with independent approaches were redeployed to teach in the area, and when the department moved from an institution in the advanced education sector to a university, there were substantial pressures, which were strongly resisted by some, to focus more on research and developing a public profile rather than on teaching.

Nevertheless, a stage of maturity has now been reached in the development of the school and a critical mass of staff and students who have experienced a new approach has been established, which means that whatever changes in teaching and learning are introduced in the future, a move to unilateral, teacher-directed approaches is unlikely. A culture has been created that places a high value on the forms of negotiated learning which have evolved over time. Students enrol because they expect these forms of learning (although they don't fully appreciate the consequences for them when they start!), and staff regard the mix of activities as normal.

A sign of the confidence which has now been achieved occurred in 1993 with the adoption by staff of an explicit teaching philosophy for the school. The statement of this philosophy includes *inter alia* the following principles:

- respect for individual learners and the explicit use of learners' experience
- respect for the cultural and linguistic diversity of learners
- learners taking responsibility for their own learning
- critique of one's own practice as teacher and as learner
- collaboration between staff and students and the negotiation of specific learning tasks
- cooperative rather than competitive approaches in which learners are encouraged to set and attain goals which extend themselves
- the promotion of critical thinking and a questioning of taken-for-granted assumptions.

It is recognized that:

- learners have the right to participate in decisions made about their learning
- learners are necessarily creators of knowledge as well as consumers of knowledge created by others
- notwithstanding differences of roles and responsibilities, students and staff are peers as educational practitioners

- independent learning is developmental and students have different requirements at different stages

- educators need to develop and be able to articulate their own theoretical and value bases

- theory and practice inform each other, interrelate with each other and are in a continual state of tension

- effective practice needs to be critically reflexive.

FEATURES OF THE COURSES

What are the features which characterize the teaching practices of the school? The following summarizes the main features of courses which promote independent study and flexible learning.

Use of learning contracts

The widespread use of contract learning at all levels means that learning tasks which are meaningful to each student are negotiated with staff members and that through this process students become committed to them (Knowles, 1975). This tailoring courses and subjects to individual needs is a form of 'liberating structure' (Torbert, 1978) that provides a framework in which students can operate, but which does not unilaterally define the specific features of learning tasks in which they engage. The use of contracts is ubiquitous and is the predominant form of assessment in most courses. For example, students in the bachelors course typically complete over 50 learning contracts by the time they graduate. In the light of the fact that the school is probably one of the heaviest users of learning contracts anywhere, a research programme on the use of learning contracts has been underway since 1991. Of the many findings, one of the most significant is that there was overwhelming support among staff and students in the school for the use of learning contracts as a major feature of courses (Anderson *et al.*, 1994).

Class sizes do not reduce by level

Class sizes are limited to maximize participation. Unlike the practice in many traditional courses, there is not a pattern of large first-year classes with very small final-year ones. Class size is often larger in the masters than at beginning undergraduate level. This is based upon the assumption that more intensive work with students is needed early on when they are developing their study skills. More experienced students should need less assistance. This is a common assumption in many of the teaching innovations in higher education which emphasize student responsibility (see, for example, Little and Ryan, 1991). The largest class in any subject in any course in 1994 was

40, although 20 is more common. Even then, students spend time in smaller groups as well.

Balance of individual, group and class-based study

'Teaching' involves participative activities consistent with adult learning principles, rather than formal lectures. In addition to learning contracts, the following are in common use in undergraduate and postgraduate courses:

- student study groups
- use of a range of reflective strategies (Boud and Knights, 1994)
- group work
- peer teaching and learning
- student pair work
- one-to-one staff-student advising
- one- and two-day intensive workshops.

Some lectures are given, but this is far from the predominant mode. Individual staff use a number of other strategies in their own classes, including self-assessment (Boud, 1992; in press), group-negotiated learning, etc.

Ungraded assessment and quality feedback to students

All assessment is designed to result in feedback to students; no examinations are used and there are no assessment procedures used exclusively for summative purposes. Forms of assessment that do not result in feedback tailored to the individual (for example, multiple choice tests) are avoided.

The use of ungraded assessment places emphasis on qualitative feedback to students rather than grades which do not communicate information about quality in learning. The absence of any hint of comparative (normative) assessment means that there are increased opportunities for group work and for cooperative activities between students.

ORGANIZATIONAL ARRANGEMENTS

In addition to the teaching and learning approaches discussed above, flexible learning is promoted by a number of other organizational arrangements.

Block teaching

The school offers two of its courses (the Diplomas in Adult Education, Aboriginal and the Graduate Diploma in Adult Education, Basic Education) as well as two stages of the bachelors course for Aboriginal students in a block mode whereby students attend intensively for a week at a time rather than meeting at a regular time each week. A version of the Master of Education in Adult Education is also offered in a combination of blocks and specially designed self-study materials. Although the block versions were designed originally for students who live outside the Sydney metropolitan area, they are increasingly providing an option for local students.

Recognition of prior learning (RPL)

The school has pioneered the systematic recognition of prior learning in Australian universities (known in the UK as assessment of prior experiential learning). It has implemented an RPL scheme for Aboriginal students and is planning to introduce a core subject in the first year of the bachelors course which will involve students identifying the learning which they bring to the course, developing learning portfolios and, if appropriate, seeking credit for existing achievements. While staff are supportive of greater use of RPL, further implementation is contingent on overcoming practical issues of funding RPL in higher education. These are linked with national policy considerations and are not being resolved quickly. The work on RPL has been acknowledged more widely and a team from the school prepared the national position paper on this topic for the Australian Vice-Chancellors' Committee (Cohen *et al.*, 1994).

Open learning

A full open learning version of the Diploma in Adult Education (Training)was developed for Telecom Australia and has been offered in Telecom workplaces throughout the country. Experience in preparing the open learning version is leading to the progressive development of subjects in this mode for on-campus students.

SOME INDICATIONS OF QUALITY

It is unusual to obtain a summative measure of effectiveness in this area, but in 1992 the courses of the school were subject to evaluation as part of a regular five-yearly faculty review. This evaluation was conducted independently of the school and used the course experience questionnaire, an instrument developed as part of the National Performance Indicators Study (Ramsden, 1991). This instrument is notable as one of the few which has been validated against measures of student learning, and Australian norm data are available. It also has a stronger theoretical base than many course evaluation measures and, appropriately, places a particular emphasis on independent study.

Alumni and current students were surveyed using this instrument. The outcomes were striking. The overall ratings of the courses offered by the school exceeded the national range of norm data for education schools on 18 out of 25 possible data cells that could be considered. Particularly high ratings were achieved on the scales which related to student independence, appropriate assessment and appropriate workload.

Recognition of the work of the school in fostering student learning was given by the school receiving the 1993 UTS Award for Excellence in Support of Student Learning which is made annually by the university to a department or school. Externally, recognition of the undergraduate course occurred through it being selected as a case study in good practice in promoting lifelong learning in a national study of the role of undergraduate education in lifelong learning (Candy *et al.*, 1994a).

FACTORS INFLUENCING THE DEVELOPMENT OF INDEPENDENT APPROACHES

That the school has been successful in its quest to institutionalize independent study is now clear. But what are the key factors which have brought about the present emphasis? Educational innovations are created and sustained through a mix of factors. Some of these factors are potentially open to manipulation and can be commended to others. However, others are a function of unique circumstances operating in a given context at a given point in time. Also, the factors which help establish a new approach are not necessarily the same as those required to sustain it. Many innovations are initiated, but few last over time.

Factors positively influencing the present developments have included the following:

- The fact that the school was operating in the field of adult education which, in rhetoric at least, is committed to the values of self-directed learning. There is a tradition of scholarship in adult education which has strongly emphasized self-directed learning as a characteristic of desirable practice.

- Self-directed learning was incorporated into the mainstream at an early stage (Boud and Higgs, 1993). Independent study was at the heart of the courses from the start – existing practices did not need to be undone, though it was necessary for staff to learn how to implement new approaches well.

- At the time at which resources for new course developments became available, there was a critical core of staff committed to and aware of independent study approaches who influenced the design of new programmes. The innovation was not identified with any one person: some movement of personnel was possible without putting the innovation at risk.

- There were sympathetic external accrediting panels who, in the early stages, were supportive of the approaches adopted. This meant that senior managers who may not have been familiar with the innovations were persuaded that the developments were sound. There was also leadership which both supported the idea of taking seriously learning – as distinct from teaching as such – and which encouraged staff who were committed to the improvement of teaching and learning to put their ideas into practice. As the adult education programmes have grown and become closely linked with the field, there has been increasing support from external bodies and former students now holding influential positions.

- Staff celebrated their achievements, made public what they had been doing and kept in close touch with the world of practice. This allows for critical debate by informed peers and acts as a counterbalance to more conservative academic influences. It was initially risky, but greatly strengthening in the long run.

While it would be easy to generate a commensurate list of negative influences, these would probably be little different from those which might be cited by academic staff in any department in order to avoid serious engagement with teaching developments. Change is hard won and in the higher education context, where management is still mostly by consent of those managed, it will always be difficult to mobilize articulate, independent professionals towards a common cooperative outcome.

One issue that raises its head from time to time is that of how to provide resources for independent study. While moves towards independent study that are prompted principally by cost-cutting considerations have never been successful, most independent study initiatives operate at the same resource level or less than conventional teaching (see Stephenson, 1988, for an example of operating a major programme with fewer resources). Resources will influence the specifics of change, but not the need or direction.

Innovative approaches need to be sustained over time if they are not to regress to some tolerated convention. While the importance of having leadership which supports initiatives continues, and is likely to be more significant than ever, other factors have started to emerge as important:

- Recruitment of staff who are sympathetic to the innovation and who are attracted to the school for what it has achieved.

- Ongoing renewal of enthusiasm to avoid the innovation being taken for granted and teaching practices regressing into pale imitations of the original. Staff development to induct new staff and to encourage existing staff becomes no less important as time passes.

● Related to this is the instigation of quality assurance mechanisms which are consistent with the character of the innovation rather than standardized forms which might be applied in any department.

● Protection of areas with high quality educational programmes from erosion by institutional rationalizations which might dilute staff commitment.

DISCUSSION IN THE LIGHT OF DEVELOPMENTS ELSEWHERE

In considering what the experience at UTS offers to the current British situation, it is immediately apparent that context dominates all. The least important aspect of the context of these innovations is the formal differences in systems between Australia and the UK. Local factors and the overall climate towards change are far more important. Almost all of the developments described above were responses of a group of people to the unique situations in which they found themselves. The particular form of the responses was shaped by the nature of the institution in which they occurred, the limited but redeployable resources which were available and the overall policy climate in Australian higher education at the time. They all occurred within the context of a field of practice, relatively new to higher education, establishing and creating itself in a way which consciously distinguished itself from related areas such as teacher education. While there were many differences of perception among staff, a common thread was that courses for adult educators should be quite different from those for teachers, especially the courses for teachers in the technical and further education system which were then being taught by colleagues in the same building. (Ironically, this perception is currently being revised as elements of the practices described here are currently being introduced into courses for vocational teachers.)

It would be considerably more difficult to institute comparable changes in well-established disciplinary areas as there are so many more vested interests among teaching staff. In professional areas, expectations of professional bodies need to be taken into account, and a change in these has often provided a useful impetus for innovation of the kind described here.

Unlike many of the UK initiatives, changes were not driven by the existence of a formal change agenda set external to the universities or by funding stimulus, for example through the Enterprise in Higher Education Initiative and other projects of the former UK Employment Department. At UTS there was no project funding until the very late stages of the innovations and this funding was given mainly to document practices that were already well-established.

The most auspicious circumstances for sustaining major moves towards independent study which have emerged from examining the case of adult education at UTS appear to be:

- courses established in a new field or sub-field

- few existing staff who 'own' the territory and have strong conservative views about what and how they should teach

- resources are redeployed from elsewhere, for example, to release key staff during the development stages

- ongoing cost structures which fit within the norms of the institution (that is to say that they are no more expensive than conventional courses)

- staff who are committed to find ways of teaching that are appropriate to the students and to the field, and who are able to let go of some of their existing practices

- senior staff who may not be actively involved in the innovation themselves, but who can protect it in its early stages and who are 'street-wise' to the internal institutional politics that can undermine new developments

- progressive exposure of the innovation to external scrutiny, both so that the institution becomes known for a particular approach and to enable the innovation to be critically examined at the stage at which staff might become complacent about it.

Not all of these factors can be present in other contexts. In particular, the first of these is rarely an option. Nevertheless, there are notable innovations within the context of traditional subject areas which involve larger-scale change than that discussed here, for example, agriculture at the University of Western Sydney, Hawkesbury (Bawden, 1985), and medicine at Harvard Medical School (Moore, 1991). There is no substitute for a group of staff who are able to work together to revise and revise again their approaches to reach a state where they are able to make a significant impact on their students' learning.

THE FUTURE

Of course, there is no guarantee that the approaches described in this chapter will continue in the same way into the future. At the time of writing, the School of Adult and Language Education had just amalgamated with a larger school (mainly responsible for training teachers in the technical and vocational education system) which has a somewhat different teaching philosophy. It is likely that the kind of innovations described here will continue in many areas, but it will interesting to see what will prevail when new courses which cross the two previous schools are developed and taught.

Mobilizing over 60 full-time academics to the kind of teaching practices discussed here is a substantial challenge. It would be naive to believe that decisions will necessarily be made on the grounds of educational arguments and demonstrated success. Deeper values will surface and emotional commitments to existing practice will be strong on all sides.

Hopefully, a story which celebrates the next phase of development will be recounted in a few years time. Until then, a number of enthusiastic people will be engaged with a potentially more difficult task than just using independent modes with students. Spreading this innovative work to their colleagues will involve putting into practice much of what this approach embodies.

Chapter 12

First steps towards the virtual university

Richard Freeman, Suzanne Robertson and Michael Thorne

STRATEGIES

The flexible learning approaches with which we have been largely concerned at Sunderland include open learning (print and non-print based), telematics (including broadcast and non-broadcast media), and computer-assisted learning. At the University of Sunderland, we see flexible learning as one of the mechanisms which can help us fulfil our mission. We see it as a means both of improving the quality of the learning experience and as a means of building the virtual university (or, as some would prefer, the university without walls), thereby enabling us to provide access to our curriculum for all kinds of individuals who would not otherwise be able to participate in higher education. Also, we have succeeded in producing packages which are now being used by a considerable number of companies and universities both in the UK and abroad.

Starting with an overarching teaching and learning development strategy, we have now agreed complementary strategies for broadcasting, information services and IT. Such has been the level of success in involving academic staff with these strategic developments that for the last two years more than 200 colleagues have participated in a programme of internal and external workshops and keynote talks at our, now annual, whole-university internal teaching and learning conference. We have also involved staff from our franchise colleges in these events as well as in the staff development activities described below. Many university staff are now publishing the results of their work, which we have encouraged them to do through a flexible learning package entitled, *Where Shall I Publish My Article?*

At Sunderland, academic activity is organized into eight schools – there are no faculties. The teaching and learning development strategy said: that we would like to see students empowered to take responsibility for much of their own learning; recognized the value of this; pointed to the range of teaching and learning and assessment methods available within each level of each programme of study; and encouraged the promotion of transferable skills. It also set a performance measure in terms of the old government inspectors' quality ratings, although these are now irrelevant, given the replacement of the professional inspectors by the well-intentioned amateurs of the Higher Education Funding Council (England) teaching quality assessment exercises.

Each of the eight academic schools has appointed a principal lecturer to lead and coordinate teaching and learning in that school. They work with the Pro Vice-Chancellor to ensure that each school produces and implements a school strategy for the development of teaching and learning, including whole-school events to focus on specific issues. These principal lectureships are a clear signal that teaching and learning is rewarded in the university.

More recently we have invited applications from lecturers and senior lecturers for a number of two-year teaching fellowships . These are intended both to give recognition to excellence in teaching and learning and/or curriculum development and to enable the wider dissemination of innovations within the university and across school boundaries. Teaching fellows are appointed for up to two years, to continue their successful innovation within their own school and to help at least two other schools successfully engage with that innovation. Teaching fellows receive the equivalent of three additional salary increments for the duration of their fellowship. The objectives to be achieved during each fellowship are agreed in advance and progress is reviewed by a Pro Vice-Chancellor every six months up to the end of the fellowship. Continuation of the fellowship up to the maximum two years is dependent on satisfactory reviews. Those who are currently readers, professors, or principal lecturers are not eligible to apply, since the fellowships are seen as a means by which unpromoted staff may establish a case for promotion.

Applications had to consist of an up-to-date cv, and a statement in not more than four sides of A4 describing:

- key achievements in either curriculum development or teaching and learning and details of the innovation which would be developed and disseminated during the teaching fellowship;

- a case for the excellence of the innovation;

- the objectives to be achieved during the teaching fellowship;

- suggestions of two other schools in which the innovation would be progressed.

CORE ACTIVITY

In order to underpin school-based activity, we have established a learning development services unit which works with schools to develop flexible learning, focusing on print but embracing IT, audio and video. The learning development services unit is closely monitored to make sure that it does not develop a life of its own, as that kind of thing so often can, by becoming a research institute rather than a curriculum support service. The last thing we want is an outfit which is well known in the conference world but has only marginal effect internally.

It is also the job of learning development services to ensure that central financing for materials development, whatever the medium, is spent strategically. Thus, we would either expect the investment to affect a large number of students or to move us forward in a new direction which offers a strong promise of a return on the investment. We do not want innovation in teaching and learning to be regarded as an extra on top of the 'normal' curriculum, nor as something for a minority of students, nor as a cranky thing in which only a minority of staff participate.

STAFF DEVELOPMENT

Of course, one of the best ways of ensuring that the use of flexible learning enhances the learning experience rather than detracting from it is through staff development. This is another respect in which our model at Sunderland singles itself out. In addition to very significant sums of money being spent on staff development in the schools themselves (each school is expected to organize a series of internal events as well as to send staff away to appropriate teaching and learning conferences), we also run a massive institutional staff development programme which last year contained over 300 courses for all kinds of staff, with two major themes focusing on changes in teaching and learning and related issues. In the coming year we will spend more than a quarter of a million pounds in this way – and that's without counting the school-based investment in staff development. Here are just a few examples of the courses available in the last academic year:

- Open Learning Programme
- Writing open learning materials
- Reviewing open learning materials
- Writing a specification for open learning development
- Developing computer-based learning materials
- Developing media-based learning
- Producing tailored texts
- Writing study guides
- Multiple-choice questions and computer-marked assessment
- School-specific team workshops
- Flexible learning with large classes

- Servicing the mature student
- Supporting independent learning
- Independent learning using student teams
- Negotiated learning using learning contracts
- Problem-based learning
- Independent fieldwork
- Developing students' independent learning skills
- Making use of broadcasting technology
- Electronic information sources and uses.

Thus, the first encounter a member of staff may have with flexible learning might be in one of these staff development sessions. He or she will explore the potential and possibly have a go at writing a section of flexible learning material. If successful, this may lead to school-based sessions in which whole groups of staff experiment further before deciding that flexible learning may benefit aspects of the curriculum for which they have responsibility.

Until recently our staff development model was focused on courses. Soon we will be using a new model which will involve:

- offering a narrower range of topics and trying new times of delivery to make them more convenient for academic staff to attend;
- inviting bids from academic staff as individuals or as programme or subject teams for funds to attend conferences or bring in external consultants to assist programme or subject teams in achieving their teaching and learning goals;
- organizing a series of directed visits to other institutions to inspect reported models of good practice and to learn from them at first hand, backed up by customized staff development sessions where appropriate.

The new model encourages staff teams to decide where they might want to take their teaching programmes, or to identify some new directions to take and then to seek out staff development support to facilitate it.

MODELS FOR MATERIALS DEVELOPMENT

In the early stages of materials development, buying in existing material is the best option so long as the staff involved will be flexible about minor differences in approach and be honest (non-defensive?) in their appraisal of material created elsewhere. Locating good material can be expected to be cheaper than starting from scratch but there is still a non-trivial cost in locating it. Actually, there seems to be surprisingly little British high quality flexible learning material, even in print, apart from Open University products.

Other models include employing outside writers and project managers and staff being seconded to produce developmental packages. Each school is expected to commit the equivalent of one full-time lecturer to learning development activity.

INDUCTING AND SUPPORTING LEARNERS

Having produced the material, then come the hard bits: inducting learners to use the flexible approach (an aspect all too easily ignored but with appalling consequences if it is) and putting in place a structure to support learners as they learn. Our approach to both these hard tasks has been empirical and we continue to react to circumstances.

It is quite hard to get lecturers to think about support in the flexible learning context. This can be because either they have too much faith in learning materials or they think the university wants to use materials to reduce tutor support. The true position is that the university fully recognizes the limitations of learning materials by themselves and is well aware that the extent and quality of learner support is crucial to student success.

The positive way to look at the support issue is to recognize that using learning materials opens up two possibilities. First, students are freed to take more responsibility for their own learning. With materials, what and how they learn depends much more on them than it does with timetabled lectures. Second, materials allow lecturers to use their contact time with students in more varied and creative ways. Freed from the need to be conveyors of information, lecturers can shift to being promoters and managers of learning through workshops, tutorials, surgeries and so on.

Once the tutoring opportunities of flexible learning are recognized, plans have to be laid to take advantage of those opportunities. For example, learning materials can be designed in a way which tries to eliminate tutor contact (the so-called 'teacher-proof' approach) but they can also be designed to promote tutor and student contact. In other words, a good support system will be one which has been developed alongside the materials, not one which has been tacked on as an afterthought.

All this implies a considerable change of role for tutors, which in turn implies the need to support and develop the tutorial function alongside the materials development function. Tutors, for example, need to be helped to:

- move from an information giving role to a learning management role;
- develop ideas for small group and workshop tasks which complement the students' individual work with materials;

- develop approaches for promoting independent learning in their students;

- be proactive, not just to wait until learners say they have a problem;

- develop a range of skills in giving feedback through written comments, on the telephone or by computer conferencing.

Our experience has also shown that learners need special support in making the transition to flexible learning. In one school's review of its first year of flexible learning activity, it was clear that a certain group of students had considerable reservations about flexible learning. The principal manifestation of this reservation was their saying 'But you still haven't told us why we are doing this flexible learning'. (Doubtless they had been told but it was clear that the method of telling had not been successful.) More seriously, the student comments indicated a feeling that flexible learning had been selected to (a) cut costs and (b) let lecturers off the hook of teaching. Not only were both these views false, but the positive reasons for undertaking flexible learning had somehow passed them by.

What this and other experiences demonstrate is the need to be much more active and thorough in inducting students into flexible learning. This will now happen at two levels. First, from September 1995, programme leaders were able to have their new students' work on a two-hour supported flexible learning package which gives an induction to learning at the University of Sunderland. This workshop addresses issues of teaching and learning styles and enables students to explore some of the benefits of working from materials and working in small groups. Student reaction to a pilot version of this workshop has been extremely positive.

Second, each flexible learning course will need to include a more considered induction element. For example, one course that was offered for the first time in autumn 1994 includes a two-hour induction workshop during which students will carry out sample activities from the course and reflect on how they intend to take advantage of the flexibility within it.

There is also the need to recognize that students are not all the same. This is a truism but one to which we often fail to respond. Just as we give the same lecture to all students, irrespective of their personal learning styles, so a materials-based course may force a common approach on to a heterogeneous group of students. There are many dichotomies for classifying students: deep versus surface learners; lone versus social learners; 18-year-olds and mature students. Good support systems will be ones in which tutors are able to adapt what they offer to match these student variations.

Several universities which have got off to a good start with flexible learning development are now contemplating dropping the name 'open learning' because of the baggage the name carries with it – in particular the fear it can raise that we wish to make all universities into distance teaching universities. As we shall point out later, in order to help certain groups of students, we believe most universities will eventually want to offer some distance teaching, be it print-based or computer mediated. But the whole point of having students on campus is to afford them face-to-face contact. What frustrates us is that so much of this is spent on pouring knowledge from one vessel to the other rather than allowing the students access to personal insights on their own understanding from staff who have far more to give than just knowledge. Good support structures for flexible learning define non-knowledge-transmission activity as the norm and hence upgrade the learning experience. But, as is known from the Open University, unless done on a massive scale, the necessary support is not cheap.

At Sunderland, we are trying to come at it from the other direction, however. Given the available staff resource and appropriate guarantees that the intention is not to decrease the total teaching resource for the cohort under consideration but rather to spend what is available more effectively, one of our models has been to start from scratch and divide the time up creatively to support best learning from the materials. This in turn has led to a variety of models including regular surgeries, tutorials with a maximum of ten students (affordable because it was decided that this was a better way to use the available time than for lectures), and simply asking students to turn up to things called 'lectures' during which the materials are worked through.

BROADCASTING STRATEGY

Complementing our teaching and learning development strategy, our strategy for broadcasting interprets the term in the widest sense and embraces the production, use and transmission of video, audio and multimedia materials, TV and radio systems, satellite and cable TV, video conferencing, internal TV networks and facilities, radio broadcasts and networked multimedia. It has been developed to ensure that the university is aware of and in a position to exploit the opportunities that broadcasting offers to extend and enhance our mission – serving students, serving industry, serving the community. Not least because the costs of our more ambitious ideas will be high, it puts considerable emphasis on making partnerships with the communications industry, other universities worldwide, and with other key information providers.

'Low tech' use of broadcasting media need not be expensive. We see student involvement in the production of video and audio material as empowering students as learners. We have a vision of a learning environment in which a student's cheap and cheerful video or audio tape is as acceptable as an essay – even in science and engineering disciplines – because the medium will force them to think about what they are learning in different ways. Our campus-based commercial radio station WearFM is already acting as a major stimulus to staff and students to work in this way.

WearFM is also important for the delivery of flexible learning. In her chapter in the forthcoming book, *Flexible Learning Strategies in Further and Higher Education*, Virtue Jones has given a candid account of our successes and difficulties. Briefly, we have run a raft of pre-foundation courses (covering topics as diverse as child psychology and chemistry) in order to target groups of listeners who might become excited enough in the topics to consider further study either with us or one of our partner colleges. One of the objectives was to widen the audience for our Open Learning van which forms one part of our educational outreach work in the City of Sunderland.

Back inside the university, we have already had one round of the broadcasting development initiative which invited competitive bids from colleagues for financial support to use broadcasting to enhance mainstream curriculum. Such 'buckshot' strategies are notorious for unpredictable returns on investment but in this case almost every project has given us a good return. Several of the projects have resulted in flexible learning materials which are now in the course of being handed over to commercial publishers. And the initiative will be repeated.

The strategy also sees cable and satellite TV networks as offering the means of breaking down the walls of the university, be it through relatively sophisticated broadcast programmes or through simple recordings of teaching sessions. The latter can offer a great deal to those students simply not able to get into the university. There are problems to be overcome with both cable and satellite TV, however, so these are longer-term developments with which we need to start getting to grips now.

On the one hand, until there is more than one source of inexpensive satellite transmission for education, developments in that direction will remain more in the research domain than a mainstream activity. On the other hand, the rate of build and take-up of cable TV locally and nationally remains patchy and slower than predicted, although the simultaneous installation of phone facilities with cable TV lines is enhancing the interactive possibilities. Nationally, we have found what is happening in the use of cable TV in education to be generally disappointing, although activities in the US and Europe are exciting to say the least. Consequently our short- and medium-term goals involve small-scale pilot activity and targeting markets very carefully.

INFORMATION SERVICES STRATEGY

Within our information services strategy we recognize and look to unleash the exciting potential of electronic databases and information resources based on CD-ROM. Through cautious but increasing reliance on electronic document delivery and a strategy of access rather than holdings, we aim to move to the kind of library provision which must underpin flexible, student-centred curriculum delivery. As with much other IT, one of the problems here is that often students are more aware of the benefits of electronic information sources than staff. Which takes us back to staff development.

We also need a more flexible and responsive model of learning support than that provided by the traditional library. We therefore have plans for one major resource centre in each of our eight academic schools to underpin independent learning in a manner complementary to library provision. Four of these are by now very well established and the rest are fledglings. Two massive new resource centres have been furnished by the conversion of an entire floor of a tower block and the opening of our new campus.

It is important to emphasize the relationship between the different types of learning resource provision. If all the students studying a module have the same predictable need for support, then it is usually the lecturer's job to provide it. If some students have a predictable need under certain circumstances (for example, because they have been ill and need to catch up, or they find a topic especially difficult or interesting), then they should seek what they need in a resource centre. If the learning requirement is unpredictable – the obvious example of this is if they are undertaking a project – then they should go to the library.

Great strides are being made in the development of information services provision to support flexible learning. 'Self-issue' is installed and running at one site and will soon be extended to others. Our franchise colleges are being connected to the university's IT network so that students can access the library computer system from their nearest FE college and are thus able to consult the catalogue, reserve and renew loans, and spin any networked CD-ROMs. We are shortly to make available an on-line inter-library loan request system.

Of course, the more facilities you provide, the more help students will need to exploit these facilities. To start them off well, we put all new students through a print-based flexible learning library induction package with book token prize incentives for completing the assignments it contains.

IT STRATEGY

Coming finally to our IT strategy, it is of course crucial to ensure that all students have minimal competence with IT facilities. That is what we mean by 'IT for all' and it is being delivered by a cross-institutional computer literacy programme, which this year reached 1,500 students through our microcomputing skills open learning pack. But the most effective use of IT to empower students as learners will, in our view, be when it grows out of the students' main curriculum. Hence there is a desire to involve IT in as many aspects of our curriculum as is sensibly possible. The strategy addresses the infrastructure (enhanced campus network capabilities, a centralized optical mark reading facility for assessments, etc), but problems will remain after that, the main one of which is cost.

The production of computer-assisted learning (CAL) material is expensive. Unless you are prepared to accept a very behavioural style of interaction with the learner, it is *very* expensive. And unless it is very behavioural there is no real reason to suppose that the costs of supporting learners using it will be less than that for print-based flexible learning.

We can only have seen the tip of the iceberg in terms of the totals of TLTP-funded material in production to date (see also Chapters 8 and 9) but we would have to risk being controversial by saying that what we have seen is very largely behavioural. It has no doubt been produced by enthusiasts for the technology. But the models of learning represented by what we have seen are really quite impoverished in the higher education context. On this evidence we really don't seem to have learned any lessons at all from the national development programme for CAL in the 1970s and the microelectronics education programme in the 1980s. We would be delighted if someone could furnish evidence to the contrary.

One way of reducing the cost of good material would be to agree a national university curriculum so that the potential number of students for a module is in several tens of thousands a year. That is how the Open University balances its books. But would colleagues be prepared to accept a national curriculum? Given the UK HEFCE teaching quality assessments, is a national curriculum unavoidable or maybe even desirable?

Despite our concern that the educational advantages justify the increased costs, CAL has its champions within Sunderland. There are several non-behavioural CAL and multimedia projects which contribute to core curriculum activity, ranging from looking at and understanding sculpture, to a complete revamp of the mathematics curriculum to make it almost entirely a laboratory activity rather than a pencil-and-paper one. We have just completed an exciting project with British Telecom in the use of video and desktop conferencing for tutor support of flexible learning material. There have been surprises but there is little doubt about the potential of video and desktop conferencing to make the virtual university concept a reality, if we can only realize it. As a result, we are committed to piloting mainstream developments in the near future based on this experience. But going back to monkey and bananas learning isn't going to move any university significantly forward.

RESEARCH

What surprises anyone working in this area is the relative lack of research work to help guide our efforts. We initially promised a review of some of the questions that need answering. Since then however, a recent conference, Educational and Cultural Barriers to Open and Distance Learning, organized by the flexible learning centre at the University of Sheffield has been circulating a draft research agenda for flexible and distance learning which we can only endorse. It really does raise the issues with which those charged with implementing flexible learning programmes need help.

THE WAY FORWARD

We are already working vigorously on the implementation of the strategies outlined in this chapter. The overriding aim is to start from the curriculum and progress outwards. To a certain extent progress is limited by resources, but perhaps the most powerful determiner of the speed at which we will progress and the quality of the result is the general level of support among university colleagues, be they in the academic schools or in the service departments. So far this support has been second to none. Indeed, we must conclude by saying that experience suggests that our way forward is by working together across the university and we are most grateful to all who contributed so ably.

Chapter 13

Change in two academic cultures

Jane Pearce, Ron Stewart, Phil Garrigan and Steve Ferguson

The research outlined in this chapter arises out of an action research project based in the department of education at the University of Liverpool. A major element of the project's work is monitoring the development and implementation of flexible learning techniques through syndicate group work within undergraduate courses of professional study. For a number of years the project team had been developing and using these methods in the training of teachers (Pearce *et al.*, 1992) and the current project extends this experience and enables us to monitor the development and implementation elsewhere.

In our research we have been able to explore what happens when attempts are made to transfer a particular system of learning – syndicate group work – from one academic 'culture' to another. By 'culture' we mean the embedded or rooted systems, beliefs and structures which form the ideological basis for the department's work. We have found that the culture of a department or an institution is a highly significant factor in determining the outcome of an innovation in the area of teaching and learning. What we have found is that if changes are to become embedded in a particular culture, then the culture itself has first to be understood.

The two cultures on which we will base our discussion are very different and have been considerably conditioned by the degree of change to which each has been exposed. The first is the culture which operates in a department of education and specifically within the secondary PGCE, a one-year course of professional teacher-training for postgraduate students. During the last ten years staff on this course, including the members of the project team, have made major changes to the methods of course delivery The other culture is that of a school of architecture which is responsible for the course of professional training for architects, albeit at an undergraduate level. Unlike the PGCE, the content of the course and its learning outcomes had not been subject to heavily prescriptive changes.

At the core of the innovation developed by the project team within the department of education was 'syndicate group learning'. A syndicate group is a small group of learners given responsibility for organizing and supporting each other's learning with the help of a tutor. The system we evolved is based on the use of 'study packs' containing various resources including written information, video and audio evidence, problem-solving activities and case studies devised by tutors. The tutor's main role is as a consultant for students who work independently in consistent groups.

With hindsight, we know that this particular innovation was easy to embed in the culture of the PGCE. Group work of varying kinds had been a feature of the programme for at least a decade; the innovation was introduced in a culture which was already well-used to change; the impetus for change came from within, from the tutors already involved in teaching the course; and it arose out of a realization that change was needed and would be for the better. Parallel with the introduction of syndicate group methods was the development of assessment procedures which could be identified by external agencies as valid measures of a student's work and professional development. When we began to work with another department the context was different.

Our work with the school of architecture at Liverpool University began with the introduction of syndicate group learning to first-year undergraduates. Senior staff in the school of architecture welcomed our proposal to introduce syndicate group methods. They had felt that teaching needed to reflect recent changes in the architect's role in society – specifically that less individualistic, more cooperatively-based learning would help to equip students for new professional realities. Department of education tutors were invited by senior staff to collaborate with first-year tutors in architecture in developing appropriate group work linked to projects. However, it was made clear from the start that there was little sense that change was urgent. Rather, the innovation was seen as exploratory – an interesting experiment. It was soon to become apparent too that the attachment to traditional values of individualism in relation to artistic creativity was strong, most clearly demonstrated by a lack of enthusiasm for formal assessment of a student's group-based work. As one would expect, some tutors espoused the proposed changes more enthusiastically than others, and differences soon emerged in how they embraced their new roles. Interestingly though, all the tutors involved were part of a common school culture, being either long-established teachers there, or postgraduate teachers who had come up through the school.

The architecture tutors, in collaboration with us, focused on one course within the first year undergraduate programme. The logic for this was to introduce new methods at the outset so that new undergraduates would not be able to have an 'old' pattern upon which to base a resistance to what they might otherwise perceive to be 'new'. The changes introduced syndicate group work to the studio project, a compulsory part of an architectural degree constituting 60 per cent of the year's assessment. The studio project takes place in a 'workshop' environment. Students carry out design projects under the close supervision of a tutor and an ongoing critique of the students' work is at the heart of the process.

An introductory phase to introduce group work methods was devised for the initial days of the studio project. Then group work was introduced in the first topics concerning the analysis of buildings, the analysis of a site, and the mapping of an urban area. The introduction of syndicate group methods required a restructuring of the delivery of the course materials but the broad content and purpose of the studio project course remained unchanged. There was to be no rethink of the whole curriculum at this stage. Changes were to be incremental.

At the risk of oversimplifying responses, we found that group work was popular with students, and was seen as professionally relevant. However, the teaching behaviour of some of the tutors constantly challenged our assumptions about the value of group work, and raised doubts about whether or not the changes were being internalized and embedded in the tutor culture. For this reason we have come to review our understanding of the processes of change in educational contexts.

Research in architecture education over the last 20 years reveals a concern about the effectiveness of the central teaching paradigm in departments of architecture – studio design work. On the one hand, Schön (1984) has singled it out as a model of reflective practice. Others have been more critical. Dutton (1987), for example, sees it as reinforcing existing power relationships and has tried to 're-form' it by setting up autonomous student groups. From a perspective of giving students more responsibility for their learning, Abercrombie carried out research on learning groups at the Bartlett School of Architecture in the 1960s (Abercrombie and Taylor, 1970). However, the nature of the change process in architecture education has not, as far as we are aware, been studied.

Most work on the implementation of educational change acknowledges its complexity as a social process. For example, when change involves planning and coordinating the work of a number of people, numerous variables come into play – perhaps as many variables as there are people involved. However, research has identified a small number of key variables playing a role in this process, and which form an interacting system that impacts crucially on the implementation process. A discussion of this that initially informed our thinking is provided by Fullan (1991), which we shall use as a framework for this discussion. Fullan identifies three sets of factors affecting implementation. First, the characteristics of the change itself: the quality of the change, the perceived need for it and its clarity and complexity. Second, local characteristics: the social conditions, the organization or setting in which people work. Third, external factors: the broader context within which change takes place such as legislation, the political climate, demographic changes such as increasing unemployment and so on.

The impact of external factors on change in education will be familiar to readers, and merits more attention than we have time for in this chapter. But we have found that the other factors – the characteristics of the change itself – and the local characteristics were not only the most influential in determining the outcomes of the change process but are also particularly relevant to our examination of culture. The nature of the change itself, although at first seeming to function independently of the culture with which it interacts, is a factor which is subtly yet fundamentally transformed by that culture. By way of illustration, we shall focus upon some of the elements of Fullan's analysis of the process of change and implementation.

THE PERCEPTION OF NEED

Innovations derived from the perceived needs of the actors are more likely to succeed than innovation imposed from outside on those who do not perceive a need for change. How does the identification of needs emerge? In order to ascertain 'need', we would suggest that members of the culture in which change takes place have to be able to engage in a process of self-analysis; that there has to be an element of consensus between the members of the culture in order to identify need; and that the need is capable of being articulated clearly. In our experience, the tutors' notion that there was a need for change conflicted with their strong belief that whatever change was implemented should not put at risk what they perceived to be the established excellence of the school. It was also made clear from the outset that any innovations were unlikely to produce significant changes in the quality of students' work since, in the words of one tutor, 'Whatever we do, they still come up with something interesting'.

CLARITY ABOUT THE AIMS AND MEANS

The need for both the change agents and the 'hosts' to have clarity about the aims and objectives of the process is important. The change agents need to be able to articulate their aims clearly and the tutors in the conjoint culture need to have a clear understanding of theirs. There is a potential for false clarity, which occurs when change is interpreted in an oversimplified way and participants assume their perceptions are shared by the others. We have recognized the need for ourselves as change agents to identify the elements of a 'host' culture as a prerequisite for the introduction of new practices and this involves us in being extremely clear about the culture and assumptions that we bring to the new setting. Greater clarity did emerge for both parties as the change was worked through.

However, with clarity came the identification of ambivalence in the architecture tutors' responses to the project's aims. While syndicate group work was acknowledged as appropriate because it could enhance student autonomy, it was also seen as a threat to individual creativity. When a group rebelled, for any reason, this was celebrated as a sign of 'creative' revolt. The initial training in group-work skills was also seen as patronizing and 'nanny-ish', in so far as it entailed the students developing social sensitivity and negotiating skills, aspects particularly valued by the project team in their work with education students.

COMPLEXITY FOR INDIVIDUALS

Any change can be examined with regard to its complexity, that is, with regard to the degree of change required of the individuals responsible for implementation. Again, this involves cultural questions such as what skills are required of the individuals involved, and to what extent alterations of beliefs and teaching strategies are necessary. This leads to questions about the flexibility of a culture, both intellectually and structurally, and also to questions about the culture for change throughout an institution. For example, well-embedded, institution-wide assessment procedures may fail to accommodate new methods of learning.

It was clearly our responsibility, as the agents of change, to ensure that the variables associated with the nature of the change itself were clearly articulated, and that allowances were made for them in negotiating innovation with members of another culture. The innovation proposed for architecture was not complex, since syndicate group work was only to be applied to about 50 per cent of the course. The activities were modifications of tasks set in previous years. Only six members of the teaching staff were involved, and one tutor was responsible for liaising with the project team. However, there was symbolic complexity, as is indicated elsewhere in this chapter, that is not necessarily easily discerned.

The second set of factors which Fullan identifies as affecting implementation – the particular (or 'local') characteristics of the context in which change is attempted – have emerged for us as clearly the most important. For Fullan, the local characteristics encompass not only the role of the teachers but also that of the community, the LEA and the principal or headteacher. For us, 'local characteristics' have become those aspects of the departmental or institutional 'culture' which impact most strongly on the processes of innovation, and which therefore require serious exploration. There are several elements, discussed below.

Rationale

Examination of the rationale of a learning culture, whether this is articulated or implicit, will provide key information about the match between the pre-existing situation and the planned innovation. For example, there was a clear conflict between the articulated rationale of tutors in the school of architecture, which involved the promotion of individual creativity and excellence, and the rationale of the project team with a background in teacher training, including as it did the wish to promote collaborative skills and team work. The introduction of syndicate group learning, one of the key aims of the project, in a culture which promoted competitiveness and individual achievement, presented us with a clear challenge. Perhaps a key element of this was the fact that while rhetorically the architecture tutors were able to accept the aims of group work as constructed by the project team, nevertheless there were difficulties for effective action.

Teaching styles

The moment when a teacher is required to adapt his or her established practice in teaching is a critical one. The greater the adaptation the more challenging, or threatening it feels. Our experience in working with tutors new to flexible learning suggests that there is a considerable difficulty in adapting to the role of facilitator of self-supporting learning groups. Generally, tutors in architecture found it difficult to adapt their usual teaching styles to the requirements of group work, and difficulties in adapting to their new roles occurred when they were present during group work, when they felt the urgency of their own academic agendas and were therefore disposed to 'take over' the sessions.

One of the factors which led to the take-over of the groups arose from tutors feeling a loss of their traditional role. Tutors had invested their prized materials when they wrote and designed the packs. This was material with which they had a strong personal engagement, and there was an element of frustration at the lack of an interpersonal structure for giving it to the students. It was, therefore, not surprising that for most tutors there was a palpable sense of loss and confusion, as well as a sense of being deskilled. A crucial factor here was that we had defined the new roles for them, based on the taken-for-granted practice in our own culture in education, and in a way that we thought was extremely clear.

We now believe that a more comfortable and productive way forward would be to provide a framework that would enable colleagues to share perceptions about practice with each other, to engage in their own evaluation of practice, and to evolve new strategies appropriate to their own culture – in short, to become their own action researchers. If we were to single out the most important factor to have affected the outcome of the project, it would be this one. The importance of the right kind of preparation and support for colleagues as they take on new roles as teachers is vital.

Structural features

A number of elements can be subsumed under this heading. First, management structures clearly play an important part. Innovation which is bottom-up and takes place within a democratic culture will differ in character from that which is governed by external top-down forces. Research suggests that the right combination of support and pressure is important: pressure without support begets resentment; support without pressure can lead to a lack of focus.

Published work strongly supports the view that strong leadership from the top, usually from deans of schools or faculties, and internalized professional needs experienced by tutors combine to produce the optimal conditions for successful implementation of problem-based learning (PBL). A recent study from Otago University in New Zealand (Schwartz *et al.*, 1994) demonstrates the failure of planned change in the medical school curriculum, centred upon PBL, when both factors were absent.

What is at issue in our work is the power of other agents from within higher education to energize and support changes. We have been involved in a form of organization for facilitating change in higher education where one department acts as consultant to another. Our experience suggests that in such a scenario issues of legitimacy, authority and control can be complex, matters which are fudged by our own rhetoric of 'collaboration' and 'consultancy'.

Another important set of structural features has to do with communication and relationships. For example, our education department operates a formal system of communication involving regular meetings and the dissemination of written reports. At the time of this work, the school of architecture had a more informal, looser communication style, with important decisions rarely being written down.

There are many more examples of cultural elements which we have found need to be interrogated if effective collaboration between different cultures is to be achieved. It should be emphasized that the existence of conflict or apparent mismatches between cultures does not preclude effective change. In fact it is only in adapting to the unfamiliar that opportunities for real innovation emerge. There is nothing new in doing what comes naturally. This view is supported by developments that have occurred since concluding the research upon which this chapter is based. Architecture tutors have since undertaken significant reforms of the curriculum and teaching methods. The innovations have arisen out of their own articulated and shared culture, informed by their earlier experiences with the project team. The reforms are owned by them and are appropriate to their own definition of need.

Was it the case that, as academics from a tradition of educational studies, we were still thinking in a 'modernist' way about the initiation and implementation of change? In other words, we found it hard to shift our belief that change occurs in a linear, sequential way. It now seems to us that there are difficulties inherent in any project which attempts to transfer a learning system from one academic culture to another, and that the nature of these difficulties becomes obvious if we accept the 'postmodern' view – that development is complex and dynamic.

There may be a useful parallel here with the reading of 'texts' in literacy theory (Doll, 1993). The postmodern view that a text can never be neutral, that it is always full of things which are there to be read whether they are intentional or not, illuminates well the situation of which we have become aware during the project's work. When the author of anything creates a 'text' (that is to say, a construct which has life independently of its creator) her or his authority is no longer guaranteed. A complex network of relations intrudes, since the viewer/reader/user will not necessarily have the same set of ideological values, understanding or experiences that the author has. Our experience has been that there are many parallels between the ways in which learning systems and texts operate, and that we, as 'authors' of a particular system, must account for the fact that the reader-text relationship is not only highly complex but also in many senses beyond our direct control. Once the text becomes available for interpretation by others, the author must expect it to carry unanticipated messages. The relationship between the user and the text is an unknown for the author: the challenge for us has been in responding to the multifarious interpretations to which our own 'text' gave rise.

Chapter 14

Student group work: a comparative study

William Johnston

Project-oriented learning strategies, no matter how varied in their origin, their scope or their purpose, share several common areas of difficulty – notably in terms of problem formulation and the relation between theory and methods of investigation. The purpose of this chapter is to explore how and where these areas of difficulty arise in two very different institutional contexts and how two different teaching and learning strategies respond to them. I would not want to suggest that the strategy adopted in either institution is the optimal solution, but rather to argue that by a careful comparison of the two approaches we can identify those features which ought to figure in any evaluation of best practice.

The basic studies programmes at Roskilde University in Denmark form the first two years of every student's initial studies at the university. On completion of the *Basis*, students go on to two or more further years of advanced study for the award of the master's degree. There are three different basic studies programmes: in the natural sciences, the social sciences and the humanities. All three programmes are project-oriented, which is to say that the predominant form of activity is work in small project groups. Students engage in four self-contained group projects, one in each semester of the two years of basic study.

At Manchester we have a two-year Diploma in Higher Education (DipHE) course which recruits from a mainly local and mature student base into a range of subject areas – though mostly in the humanities and social sciences – and provides direct access, in the majority of cases, into the third and final year of a range of degree programmes across the institution. One optional first-year unit at Manchester is the group activity. This is a student-led project-oriented unit. Comparing aspects of this single, optional unit with an entire, obligatory, basic studies programme may at first glance seem somewhat spurious – these are two very different programmes operating in two very different institutional milieux. But, beneath the surface differences are some important and telling similarities. This is not entirely accidental, in that the Manchester group activity is historically based upon our understanding and appreciation of the Roskilde basic studies scheme. When the DipHE course was being designed in the early 1970s, we spent a considerable amount of time investigating alternative teaching strategies and their educational rationale. As part of this investigation we looked at the Roskilde model and attempted to import some of what we considered to be its best features into the scheme at Manchester. Any comparative analysis of the two schemes must therefore take into account the success or otherwise of this importation.

In the UK, course aims and objectives are established by a course committee or working party of interested academics with close links and interests in the proposed scheme. In Denmark, a somewhat more centralist policy operates whereby the Education Ministry specifies study regulations and guidelines which set out what the objectives of the programme shall be. According to the Ministerial Proclamation, students following the basic studies programme in the humanities will be expected to:

- acquire a knowledge of theory and methods in philosophy, communication and texts (including language and literature), history and sociology, pedagogy and psychology;

- achieve the prerequisites for analysing those functions and roles in society for which the basic studies programme is, in part, a preparation;

- develop the ability to formulate problems from an interdisciplinary point of view;

- develop the ability to relate theory and practice, and thereby critically to evaluate scientific and scholarly theories and methods;

- develop the ability to communicate the results of their study to others, including non-academic people.

Within an overall theme for the basic studies, chosen by the board of studies at the university for each new two-year cycle (the theme for 1991/2 for example being the timely one of 'The Enlightenment and Revolution' – other recent themes have been 'Text and Meaning in Culture', 'The Social Production of Meaning' and 'Mass Media and Popular Culture'), the students choose the projects with which they will work under the guidance of the teachers attached to them for the cycle.

At Manchester, the group activity unit has the following aims:

- to provide a forum for students to engage in a student-centred and student-managed group project;

- to provide an opportunity for students to engage in experiential learning;

- to develop an explicit awareness of the dynamics of groups and in particular those features that are requisites of success and those elements that constitute barriers to success;

- to demonstrate an ability to define objectives and work through collective agreement to the successful achievement of those objectives.

In the first few years of the operation of the DipHE, and following more closely the Roskilde strategy, the group activity was a compulsory part of every student's first-year programme and an overall theme for the unit was decided upon in advance by the teachers involved. These two aspects were modified by the time of the first quinquennial resubmission. Student pressure for more flexibility in their programmes had led to the abolition of the compulsion to take group activity and the group of teachers involved in the unit, feeling the constraining pressure of the given overall theme on student innovation, had quietly let drop this requirement and passed to the students the responsibility for choosing their projects without any thematic restriction by the teachers.

Inevitably, one consequence of the absence of subject-limiting guidelines has been that student groups tend to take up much of the first term establishing the precise area in which they will work. This has led in recent years to some productive disagreement between the external assessors responsible for this part of the course. One assessor, heavily committed to the scientific research model, wanted to see a return to the 'given' topic or area of investigation – principally to enable students to focus from the start on the substantive topic and to avoid 'wasting time' settling down. Another assessor felt that the processes involved in the early settling-in stage for the group were an important element in achieving the overall objectives of the unit: far from being a waste of time, these processes were an integral part of what the unit was about. Needless to say, the teachers involved were not neutral in this debate and in general they tended to see this as symptomatic of the more general tension between the concerns for process as distinct from concerns with product, a tension which is never far from the surface in any discussions about project work.

At both Roskilde and Manchester, the teacher with specific responsibility for a project group acts in a counselling/facilitating role, the exact nature of which changes as the group progresses. Table 14.1 attempts to set out, against the main stages in that progress, the nature of the activities typical of each stage, the problems which tend to be associated with those activities and the kinds of teacher involvement. While all the stages are present in the programmes at both institutions, the way in which they are explicated and emphasized shows considerable variance between the two.

The group projects can be viewed as a form of action research in that the general, underlying principles of the projects in both institutions have a close fit with the didactic principles for action research as generally conceived – that is to say, they share a problem orientation. This is, however, not a precise model in application: the problems are here identified and defined as such by the student group involved and the participants are steering the research, whereas genuine action research is primarily carried out by researchers who have a theoretical background and first-hand acquaintance with methods through previous research experience.

Table 14.1 *Stages in student group work*

Stage	Main activities	Typical problems	Typical teacher involvement
Introduction	Getting to know each other; developing a common orientation to the exercise	Learning to operate as a group; uncertainty about norms and frames of reference	Enabling a structural framework; clarification of parameters; development of appropriate climate
Choice of topic	Topic identification related to interests and values of the individual group members	Struggle for influence; choice of topic in which all are interested	Helping steer towards promising topics by raising questions and challenging
Problem formulation	Precise formulation of problems – preferably in question format	Disagreements and conflicts; limiting and focusing the topic	Bringing conflicts into the open; holding the group to its decisions
Planning and organization of activities	Making a time schedule; planning division of labour; making contacts and establishing routines	Choosing workable procedures and sticking to them	Mediation on information and contacts; reference to relevant materials
Investigation or other planned activity	Data collection and analysis; continuous evaluation and adjustment of procedures	Practical and content problems; coordination; attendance; sharing of findings/activities	Inspiring self-reflection by the group on its own processes and progress
Production of report	Decisions about form and media for presentation	Pressure of time; structuring and producing material for presentation	Moral and practical support; pointing out errors and possibilities for improvement
Evaluation	Presentation of the product and evidence of processes to the assessors on time	Practical arrangements; nervousness; involvement of all group members	Providing a realistic orientation to the presentation and assessment
Post-evaluation	Conscious reflection to develop perspectives for further study and action	Unconditional openness; willingness to admit what has been learnt	Holding the group fast to meaningful reflections and avoiding recriminations

The main problems experienced by Manchester and Roskilde students in connection with this form of action research are as follows:

- At Roskilde, in particular, there is real difficulty in allowing the emergence of the student's own definition of the problem. Where it does emerge – and it usually does in both institutions – the difficulty then is how to allow this definition to become the central focus for the development of the group's insight and knowledge. The problem is particularly acute at Roskilde because the tutors bring problems to the group for action, thereby importing some artificiality into the process of problem formulation and solution.

- Second, the students, while working with and 'solving' the problems as identified either by themselves or the client, must master theories on several levels. This is rarely totally successful and groups tend to become atheoretical, or never get to the stage of explicitly recognizing the theory behind their practices. Alternatively, they frequently take on board quite uncritically the theoretical presuppositions of the client or, indeed, their own. It is rare for the groups to arrive at the stage where they are able to discuss their project from the perspective of alternative theories – in other words to arrive at the stage of being able to integrate theory and the methods of investigation.

When students are challenged as to their understanding of the relation between theory and practice a common set of assumptions seems to emerge:

(a) a person has (or acquires) a theory;
(b) the way in which that theory should be used has to do with demonstrating that the theory fits some empirical material and that the 'solution' to the project problem reproduces or manifests the explanation provided by the theory.

In other words, students do not work on the assumption that reality can work *back* onto theory in a way which influences concept formation and clarification. They see the general in the specific but cannot see the specific affecting the general. Thus, for example, students working on a project centred on peer group attitudes to drink-driving, may bring with them into the project ideas about the way that peer group pressure affects behaviour. The project then sets out to demonstrate this. Rarely do the students sit back and examine their assumptions. Theories are sacrosanct. This way of thinking is, of course, related to the hypothetico-deductive method, but why that way of thinking is the dominant one amongst students is quite a fascinating problem.

For project work based on an action research model to become truly fruitful as a distinctive pedagogic strategy, ways need to be found to break down the students' tendency to think about problems in this way. We need to produce strategies that encourage the emergence of fractures and discontinuities in the students' way of thinking and to get them to see the relation between theory and practice in a rather more reflective way. This can be achieved by the teacher pointing out the hidden theoretical assumptions made by the group and by insisting that data which contradict these assumptions are not automatically disregarded, but should be seen as a challenge to the assumptions. Also, students need to arrive at the insight that problem definition and, indeed, their own common perception of what the problem is, are contingent upon contextual, usually social, conditions. When we achieve this in our group work projects, then we have truly arrived at something distinctive and worthwhile.

At both Manchester and Roskilde the groups are formed from very mixed cohorts of students both in terms of social background and with regard to age and experience. The DipHE course at Manchester enrols mainly mature students without traditional qualifications. At Roskilde the students are more mixed, comprising those from the *gymnasium* with a secondary school diploma studying alongside those enrolled on *dispensation*, who do not have the school-leaving certificate but who are admitted on experiential criteria. Now, while it can be agreed that all students should be encouraged to think abstractly – which is only another way of saying that they should be able to relate theory accurately and explicitly to practice in concrete situations – there is some evidence that supports the common intuition that students coming into these programmes direct from school have, by and large, already begun to learn to think abstractly, but often to do so in ways that are detached from concrete reality. On the other hand, students enrolled on the basis of 'life experience', while having the experience of concrete reality, often in considerable abundance, have not necessarily begun to think abstractly in relation to these experiences.

This latter group of students tends to steer towards projects which focus upon concrete practical problems but the danger here is that this tends to overemphasize the importance of the 'solution': students tend to become focused on product at the expense of the all-important development of critical awareness of the process.

At Roskilde, groups can easily come to see themselves in competition with one another for grades with the result that the choice of project can be affected by the fact that certain types of projects can be seen as having higher status and to be more highly valued. Super-abstract projects tend to be developed by project groups composed of students from the *gymnasium* and these groups quickly become seen by the others as super-groups. Groups preferring more concrete-based topics have felt themselves and their project to be thereby devalued.

A related issue that affects all independent study but is particularly visible in project group work, is the dubious academic worth of the product itself. In part this is the old 'depth versus breadth' controversy. As Norman Graves has put it, 'Whilst it is generally true that following a course in higher education enables a student to explore a particular subject area in depth, this is also associated with scanning the breadth of a field of study' (1993, p.93). The problems with project group work are that the project topic is frequently extremely narrow (the two examples given above both suffer from this defect) and while it will have been diligently and honestly explored, the background knowledge and understanding possessed by the students may be too limited to do justice to the topic being studied. This is a particularly serious problem for the Roskilde scheme. At Manchester, students are concurrently studying other discipline-based units which, hopefully, may provide some of the necessary background. The response to this problem is that group work – and indeed all independent study – seeks to develop general intellectual skills rather than build up a body of substantive know-ledge. While this point is well made, it often ignores the close connection between the development of a particular set of intellectual skills and the kind of disciplinary framework that one uses to solve a particular kind of problem.

One feature of the Manchester scheme which is missing at Roskilde is a mid-session visit from the external assessor. This is built into the programme as an important opportunity both for the assessor to hear how the project is going and to comment on perceived strengths and weaknesses. It also has the function of focusing the group mind at this mid-point on what is being achieved and also on what the final outcome may be. Rather like writing definitive documents for new degree proposals, the value lies principally in the fact that it forces the proposers to organize themselves and get it together in the first place! Lacking this externally imposed focus, the Roskilde groups can easily drift into crude information-gathering activities and some extensive navel-gazing, culminating in a final mad-panic rush as the deadline looms for project submission. Visiting the Roskilde campus in the weeks prior to the deadline gives the impression that finals are not far off! To a considerable extent the mid-term review at Manchester mitigates against this to the benefit of the overall objectives of the activity.

When the final results are known at Manchester the students and their tutors head for the pub. Any post-mortem is likely to be superficial and largely consist in railing against the inadequacies and general blindness of the external assessor. At Roskilde, in comparison, a formal post-evaluation session is held for each group where the tutor and students talk though what has been learnt and its consequences for further action or future study. These points are summarized in Table 14.2.

Another problem identified by Norman Graves is: 'the extent to which students tend to concentrate on topics on which they have strong views' (*op.cit.* p.94). Now of course there is a sense in which this is both desirable and inevitable. Who wants their students only to study topics in which they have no personal interest? But there is a serious problem which emerges where the group seems to achieve little more than the amassing of evidence to support their original preconceptions. As Graves puts it:

> the problem for an assessor is to decide how far the product of such...study is flawed because the student is bigoted in his (*sic*) views and incapable of seeing the other side of a case, or because he was allowed to undertake such a narrow study in the first place. (p.94)

Table 14.2 *Comparison of structural constraints on group work at Manchester and Roskilde*

	MMU	RUC
Group size	12	5
Hours/week	2	10
Topic	open	related to given theme
Formative evaluation	mid-term review	post-evaluation review
Final presentation	open	standardized A4 soft-bound document
Final evaluation	external/internal staff assessors	peer group assessment

This latter point perhaps takes us rather too far away from our immediate concerns with identifying the mechanisms and strategies which make for effective and worthwhile group project work, but the first point, that the project can be flawed, not because the outcome is inadequate or poor in itself but because the students' position is limited and one-sided and fails to place the topic within its context, is obviously not just a problem for the assessor but for the teacher and student alike.

What is very clear from the range of issues so far identified is the crucial role of the tutor in his or her relationship with the group and the importance of the various devices used to ensure effective development of the groups. At Roskilde, considerable time and effort is taken at the commencement of the semester with group formation. Enabling individual students to choose consciously and deliberately between alternative topics and, even more importantly, between groups containing different individuals whose strengths and weaknesses become known very quickly, is seen as a vital part of the process. At Manchester, groups are pre-formed by the tutors before the students meet each other. These days this tends to be done randomly, although previously it was done by trying to achieve a distribution of discipline interests within each group. Movement of individuals between groups during the early weeks at both institutions is permitted but discouraged, and by and large little movement actually occurs. The result is that at Roskilde a strong group feeling emerges quickly, especially from semester two onwards. At Manchester, the early weeks of the project are dominated by structured or unstructured mechanisms whereby the individuals in the group establish themselves as group members. At Roskilde, the operating context is one which is very supportive of group work. Group work is the norm, it is what you came to Roskilde for and other groups are operating in close daily proximity to your group. The physical surroundings are also supportive of, nay, designed for, group work, and the majority of your study time during each week is devoted to the group project. Compared with this, Manchester offers a much more arid prospect: most students on the course are not involved in group work; much of your time is spent doing other, more traditional units; and the surroundings are purpose-built rooms for holding lectures and seminars with virtually no space where comfortable, informal group discussions can take place. These obvious differences make for differences in student perception of what they are doing and in what they do. An experiment set up in 1990 to link two groups, one at Manchester and one at Roskilde, using e-mail on a common topic, proved disastrous. In part this was in consequence of external factors. In particular, the e-mail connection was horrendously unreliable and slow at the Danish end but it was also a consequence of the very different operating context within which the two groups worked. For one thing the speed at which the two groups were working was quite out of sync, since the Danes were spending almost their whole week on the topic, whereas the British met for just two hours on a Wednesday afternoon.

What this might imply for future European integration is one thing. What it implies about the relationship between course structure and institutional context, on the one hand, and the mechanisms and strategies which make for effective and worthwhile group project work, on the other, is clear enough. The lesson, which is perhaps a pretty obvious one, is that what works in one context *may* work in another but it will have to work quite differently and with very different strategies, mechanisms and indeed, results.

Chapter 15

The development of a key competence

Peter Knight and Jo Tait

We agree with the observation made by Tomlinson and Saunders (1995) that any identification of competences is an expression of a theory, albeit an implicit theory, of human capability. There are, of course, many competing theories of human capability, hence many possible lists of desirable competences. We have averred that being able to work within open and flexible learning systems, being a self-directed, autonomous learner, equipped for lifelong learning is a key competence and contributors to this volume have taken the same position. It is, however, a position that could be contested.

Having acknowledged that, we would reply that there is evidence that employers in the UK value the qualities associated with the independent learner. Moreover, such an approach to learning has been seen as educationally desirable, not least because of the power it has to encourage deep approaches to learning – approaches that are valued by educationists. In addition, the literature on professional development (see, for example, Eraut, 1994; Winter, 1995) emphasizes the importance of *continued* professional learning, which is in no small measure predicated upon the ability to be a self-directed learner. Barnett (1994) has placed similar emphasis on the significance of the development of self, which implicates the development of autonomy in learning, in his discussion of the limits of competence and of the purposes of higher education. In short, we conclude that there is a case for seeing learner autonomy as a key competence in higher education.

Contributors to this volume have identified a number of ways in which such independence might be developed: through the development of flexible learning approaches, sometimes mediated through IT; through degree schemes that allow learners to set the pace and to shape the content of their study; through projects and critical engagements with professional activity; through group work; and through Independent Studies (IS) programmes. An important theme has been that learner autonomy is not well served by an approach that assumes that it will be achieved by substituting student projects for tutor-directed courses of lectures and seminars. Contributors have pointed to the difficulties in designing flexible learning sequences; in using IT to enhance learning, rather than simply to provide activities of questionable value; in designing and running programmes that allow learners to set the pace and to select the content; in making group work work; in leading academic staff to change their approaches to their work in quite fundamental ways; in resourcing courses and programmes designed to encourage learner autonomy; and in keeping a commitment to deep approaches to learning at the fore. It has also been shown that students are not invariably happy with having to adopt ways of working that are often quite outside their academic experiences. Student resistance is a common feature of the early days of many flexible programmes designed to enhance learner autonomy: being in control, even to a limited degree, can be scary for students. To this list of difficulties might be added the problems that go with producing a system of assessment that, unlike many assessment systems, reinforces the goals of the curriculum, rather than one that reinterprets them by signalling that some goals are not valued and by implying that the acquisition and reproduction of information are the real priorities. For independent learning to flourish, assessment systems need to give weight to the processes of working as well as to their products. To do this fairly and in ways that reassure academic colleagues about the standards associated with independent learning is no easy task.

We emphasize two implications of this summary. First, where learner autonomy is a goal, then there is a shift from teaching to learning. As it is, we know that some academic staff have views of learning that lead them to adopt a transmission approach to teaching, and that substantial and sophisticated staff development work is needed if there is to be any hope of changing those beliefs (see, for example, Trigwell, 1995). Where 'teaching' is redefined as supporting learning, then achieving such changes in beliefs and helping colleagues to acquire appropriate pedagogical techniques becomes an urgent staff development matter. And, to be realistic, it is a venture that will not succeed with all academic staff.

Second, if the practices of independent learning are prized, then the curriculum needs to be designed to promote them: their development ought not to be left to chance but should be underpinned by a sequence of opportunities and academic practices that allow students to learn how to take the initiative and that help them to become better at doing so. Regrettably, there is a dearth of research that investigates how learner autonomy develops. We know that IS programmes and other planned opportunities for learners to become more self-directed do succeed, although we have a suspicion that rather more rigorous research into the outcomes of these courses would be valuable. However, we know little about the sequences of development. Nor do we know much about the learners' feelings and beliefs as they go through such courses. Our priority may be the development of learner autonomy but, because IS have often been seen as 'wacky', rather marginal programmes, the work has not been done that would help us to see what would be a good scaffolding to support the development of this competence of autonomy. Contributors to this book identify plenty of supportive practices but we lack a developmental map to guide their application.

Such difficulties notwithstanding, we commend the development of this key competence as a goal for higher education. Like most curriculum developments, it has high start-up costs, especially in terms of opportunity-costs to academic staff. Some ways of fostering learner autonomy may not lead to cost savings in either the medium- or in the long-term. The implication is that valuable though this competence is, because its development ought not to be left to chance, some cost-benefit analysis of the different ways of fostering it needs to be done by curriculum development teams.

In that analysis it should not just be the cognitive benefits that are recognized. The massive review of the effects of higher education, mainly in North America, carried out by Pascarella and Terenzini (1991), suggests that the climate of academic departments can make a substantial impact on learners' non-cognitive development: on their attitudes, values, sense of self, personal adjustment and sense of well-being. We suggest that it is in higher education's interest to learn from such departments so as to make such outcomes more widespread. We conclude that the goal of enhancing learner autonomy through the scaffolding provided by an academic environment that emphasizes learning and the learner, rather than teaching and the teacher, is a goal that promises to support such non-cognitive developments.

Promoting learner autonomy is a key competence, in our view, not simply for the cognitive benefits it brings, but because it is also tantamount to personal development.

References

Abercrombie, MLJ and Taylor, PM (1970) 'Diploma Project (1968–69)', *Architectural Research and Training*, 1, 6–12.

Ainley, P (1994) *Degrees of Difference: Higher education in the 1990s*, London: Lawrence and Wishart.

Alessi, SM and Trollip, SR (1991) *Computer-based Instruction: Methods and development*, Englewood Cliffs, NJ: Prentice Hall.

Anderson, G, Boud, D and Sampson, J (1994) 'Expectations of quality in the use of learning contracts', *Capability: The International Journal of Capability in Higher Education*, 1, 1, 22–31.

Ashby, E (1973) 'The structure of higher education: a world view', *Higher Education*, 2, 142–51.

Atkins, M (1995) 'What should we be assessing?', in Knight, P (ed.) *Assessment for Learning in Higher Education*, London: Kogan Page.

Bailey, A (1990) 'Personal transferable skills for employment: the role of higher education', in Wright, A (ed.) *Industry and Higher Education: Collaboration to improve students' learning and training*, London: Society for Research into Higher Education.

Ball, C (1989) *More Means Different: Widening access to higher education*, London: Royal Society of Arts.

Barnett, R (1992) *Improving Higher Education: Total quality care*, Buckingham: Society for Research into Higher Education and the Open University Press.

Barnett, R (1994) *The Limits of Competence, Knowledge, Higher Education and Society*, Buckingham: SRHE and the Open University Press.

Baume, D (1994) *Developing Learner Autonomy*, Birmingham: Staff and Educational Development Association.

Bawden, R J (1985) 'Problem-based learning: an Australian perspective', in Boud, D (ed.) *Problem-based Learning in Education for the Professions*, Sydney: Higher Education Research and Development Society of Australasia.

Bernstein, B (1975) *Class, Codes and Control, volume 3*, London: Routledge.

Biggs, JB (1989) 'Does learning about learning help teachers with teaching? Psychology and the tertiary teacher', *Supplement to the Gazette*, XXXVI, 1, 20 March.

Biggs, JB (1992) 'Teaching: design for learning', *Higher Education Research and Development*, 11, 1, 1–25.

Biggs, JB (1993) 'From theory to practice: a cognitive systems approach', *Higher Education Research and Development*, 12, 1, 73–85.

Black, H *et al.* (1991) *Changing Teaching, Changing Learning: A review of teaching and learning methods in secondary schools*, Sheffield: Employment Department.

Bloxham, S and Heathfield, M (1994) 'Marking changes: innovation in the design and assessment of a post graduate diploma in youth and community work', in Gibbs, G (ed.) *Improving Student Learning: Theory and practice*, Oxford: Oxford Centre for Staff Development.

Boud, D (1992) 'The use of self-assessment schedules in negotiating learning', *Studies in Higher Education*, 17, 2, 185–200.

Boud, D (1995) *Enhancing Learning through Self Assessment*, London: Kogan Page.

Boud, D and Higgs, J (1993) 'Bringing self-directed learning into the mainstream of tertiary education', in Graves, N (ed.) *Learner Managed Learning: Practice, theory and policy*, Leeds: World Education Fellowship and Higher Education for Capability.

Boud, D and Knights, S (1994) 'Designing courses to promote reflective practice', *Research and Development in Higher Education*, 16, 229–34.

British Telecom (BT) (1993) *Matching Skills: A question of demand and supply*, London: BT.

Brook, I (1993) 'Independent Study at Lancaster', *INIS*, 23.

Brookfield, S (1985) *Self-directed Learning: From theory to practice*, San Francisco, CA: Jossey Bass.

Burgoyne, J and Stuart, R (1976) 'The nature, use and acquisition of managerial skills and other attributes', *Personnel Review*, 5, 4, 19–29.

Candy, P, Crebert, G and O'Leary, J (1994a) *Developing Lifelong Learners through Undergraduate Education. National Board of Employment, Education and Training, Commissioned Report No 28*, Canberra: Australian Government Publishing Service.

Candy, P, Crebert, G and O'Leary, J (1994b) 'Developing lifelong learners', *Capability in Higher Education*, 1, 1, 22–31.

Carter, RG (1985) 'A taxonomy of objectives for professional education', *Studies in Higher Education*, 10, 2, 135–49.

Carter, R and Cooke, F (1987) 'An accelerated experience course in project engineering', *Electronics and Power*, 33, 101–4.

Casey, D (1983) 'The role of the set adviser', in Pedler, M (ed.) *Action Learning in Practice*, Aldershot: Gower.

Caul, B (1993) *Value-added: The personal development of students in higher education*, Belfast: December Publications.

Cohen, R, Flowers, R, McDonald, R and Schaafsma, H (1994) 'Learning from experience counts', in *Recognition of Prior Learning in Australian Universities*, Canberra: Australian Government Publishing Service.

Committee of Scottish University Principals (1992) *Teaching and Learning in an Expanding Higher Education System*, Edinburgh: Scottish Centrally-Funded Colleges.

Council of University Classics Departments (CUCD) (1990) *Classics in the Market Place: An independent research study on attitudes to the employment of classics graduates*, Exeter: CUCD, Department of Classics, University of Exeter.

Creanor, L and Durndell, H (1994) 'Teaching information handling skills with hypertext', *Program*, 28, 4, 349–65.

Creanor, L *et al.* (1995) *A Hypertext Approach to Information Skills: Development and evaluation*, Glasgow: University of Glasgow.

CTI (1995) 'CTI Centre Directory', *Active Learning*, 2, 65.

Dahllof, U (1991) 'Towards a new model for the evaluation of teaching', in Dahllof, U *et al.* (eds) *Discussions of Education in Higher Education*, London: Jessica Kingsley.

Darby, Sir Charles (1993) 'Quality assessment and employment satisfaction', in Harvey, L (ed.) *Proceedings of the Second QHE Quality Assessment Seminar*, Birmingham: QHE.

Dart, PC and Clarke, JA (1990) *Modifying the learning environment of students to enhance personal learning styles*, paper presented to Australian Association for Research in Education, Sydney.

Dart, PC and Clarke, JA (1991) 'Helping students become better learners: a case study in teacher education', *Higher Education*, 22, 317–35.

De Nicolo, P, Entwistle, NJ and Hounsell, DJ (1992) *What is Active Learning?*, Sheffield: Universities and Colleges Staff Development Unit.

Department of Trade and Industry and Council for Industry and Higher Education (DTI/CIHE) (1990) *Getting Good Graduates*, London: HMSO.

Dixon, M (1992) *The Uptake of IT as a Teaching Aid in Higher Education: A social science perspective*, Oxford: CTISS.

Doll, WE Jr (1993) *A Post-modern Perspective on Curriculum*, New York: Teachers' College Press.

Doughty, G *et al.* (1995) *Using Learning Technologies: Interim conclusions from the TILT project*, Glasgow: University of Glasgow.

Doyle, W (1983) 'Academic work', *Review of Education Research*, 53, 159–200.

Draper, SW *et al.* (1994) *Observing and Measuring the Performance of Educational Technology*, Glasgow: University of Glasgow.

Dressel, P L and Thompson, MM (1973) *Independent Study*, San Francisco, CA: Jossey Bass.

Driver, G *et al.* (1990) *Evaluation of the TVEI Flexible Learning Development* (internal paper), Sheffield: TEED, Employment Department.

Duffy, C, Arnold, S and Henderson, F (1995) 'NetSem – electrifying undergraduate seminars', *Active Learning*, 2.

Dutton, TA (1987) 'Design and studio pedagogy', *Journal of Architectural Education*, 41, 16–25.

Eley, M E (1992) 'Differential adoption of study approaches within individual students', *Higher Education*, 23, 231–54.

Entwistle, AC and Entwistle, NJ (1992) 'Experiences of understanding in revising for degree examinations', *Learning and instruction*, 2, 1–22.

Entwistle, NJ (1987) 'A model of the teaching-learning process', in Richardson, JTE *et al.* (eds) *Student Learning: Research in education and cognitive psychology*, Buckingham: Open University Press.

Entwistle, NJ (1992a) *The Impact of Teaching on Learning Outcomes in Higher Education*, Sheffield: Universities' and Colleges' Staff Development Unit.

Entwistle, NJ (1992b) 'Student learning and study strategies', *in Encyclopaedia of Cognitive Psychology*, Oxford: Blackwell.

Entwistle, NJ and Entwistle, AC (1991) 'Contrasting forms of understanding for degree examinations: the student experience and its implications', *Higher Education*, 22, 205–27.

Entwistle, NJ and Marton, F (1994) 'Knowledge objects: understandings constituted through intensive academic study', *British Journal of Educational Psychology*, 64, 161–78.

Entwistle, NJ and Percy, KA (1973) 'Critical thinking or conformity: an investigation of the aims and outcomes of higher education', in *Research into Higher Education*, London: Society for Research into Higher Education.

Entwistle, NJ and Ramsden, P (1983) *Understanding Student Learning*, Beckenham: Croom Helm.

Eraut, M (1994) *Developing Professional Knowledge and Competence*, London: Falmer Press.

Fowler, G (1993) 'Learner managed learning: an androgic policy for higher education?', in Graves, N (ed.) *Learner Managed Learning*, Leeds: Higher Education for Capability.

Freidlander, BZ (1975) 'Some remarks on open education', *American Educational Research Journal*, 12, 465–8.

Fullan, M (1991) *The New Meaning of Educational Change*, London: Cassell.

Furlong, J and Maynard, T (1995) *Mentoring Student Teachers*, London: Routledge.

Galton, M and Williamson, J (1992) *Groupwork in the Primary Classroom*, London: Routledge.

Gelb, M and Buzan, T (1994) *Lessons from the Art of Juggling*, London: Aurum Press.

Gibbs, G (1992a) *Improving the Quality of Student Learning*, Bristol: Technical and Education Services.

Gibbs, G (1992b) *Problems and Course Design Strategies*, Oxford: Oxford Centre for Staff Development.

Goodyear, P (1994) 'Telematics, flexible and distance learning in postgraduate education: the MSc in Information Technology and Learning at Lancaster University', *CTISS file*, 17, 14–19.

Goodyear, P and Steeples, C (1993) 'Computer-mediated communication in the professional development of workers in the advanced learning technologies industry', in Barta, BZ, Eccleston, J and Hambusch, R (eds) *Computer Mediated Education of Information Technology Professionals and Advanced End-users*, North Holland: Elsevier.

Gordon, A (1983) 'Attitudes of employers to the recruitment of graduates', *Educational Studies*, 9, 1, 45–64.

Gordon, G (1993) 'Quality assurance in higher education: progress achieved and issues to be addressed', *Quality Assurance in Education*, 1, 3, 15.

Gore, JM (1993) *The Struggle for Pedagogies*, London: Routledge.

Gore, JM and Zeichner, KM (1991) 'Action research and reflective teaching in preservice teacher education: a case study from the United States', *Teaching and Teacher Education*, 7, 2, 119–36.

Graves, N (1993) 'Assessing learner managed learning', in Graves, N (ed.) *Learner Managed Learning*, Leeds: Higher Education for Capability.

Grundy, S (1987) *Curriculum: Product or Praxis?*, London: Falmer Press.

Hammond, N *et al.* (1992) 'Blocks to the effective use of information technology in higher education', *Computers in Education*, 18, 155–62.

Hampson, E (1994) *How's Your Dissertation Going?*, Lancaster: Innovation in Higher Education Unit.

Harvey, L (ed.) (1993) *Quality Assessment in Higher Education:* Collected papers of the QHE Project, Birmingham: Quality in Higher Education Unit.

Harvey, L with Green, D (1994) *Employer Satisfaction - Summary*, Birmingham: Quality in Higher Education Unit.

Harvey, L and Knight, P (1996) *Transforming Higher Education*, Buckingham: Society for Research into Higher Education and the Open University Press.

Harvey, L and Mason, S (1995) *The Role of Professional Bodies in Higher Education Quality Assurance*, Birmingham: Quality in Higher Education Unit.

Harvey, L, Burrows, A and Green, D (1993) *Someone Who Can Make An Impression: Report of the QHE employers' survey of qualities of higher education graduates, (2nd edn)* Birmingham: Quality in Higher Education Unit.

Henry, J (1989) 'Meaning and practice in experiential learning', in Weil, SW and McGill, I (eds) *Making Sense of Experiential Learning*, Buckingham: Society for Research into Higher Education and the Open University Press.

Hodgkinson, D, (1993) 'Who wants Independent Study?', *INIS*, 23.

Hodgson, V (1984) 'Learning from lectures', in Marton, F, Hounsell, DJ and Entwistle, NJ (eds) *The Experience of Learning*, Edinburgh: Scottish Academic Press.

Hyland, T (1993) 'Professional development and competence-based education', *Educational Studies*, 19, 1, 123–32.

Johnson, D, Pere-Vergé , L and Hanage, R (1993) 'Graduate retention and the regional economy', *Entrepreneurship and Regional Development*, 5, 85–97.

Keats, DW and Boughey, J (1994) 'Task-based small group learning in large classes: design and implementation in a second year university botany course', *Higher Education*, 27, 59–73.

Kinzie, MB, Larsen, VA, Burch, JB and Boker, SM (1995) 'Net-Frog: using the WWW to learn about frog dissection and anatomy', *Proceedings of the Internet Society's 1995 International Networking Conference (INET'95)*, Honolulu: INET, (http://infoiso-corg:80/HMP/PAPER/135/html/paperhtml).

Knight, P (1985) 'Examining the licence to skill', *Curriculum* 6, 2, 36–41.

Knight, P (1995) *Assessment for Learning in Higher Education*, London: Kogan Page.

Knowles, MS (1975) *Self-directed Learning: A guide for learners and teachers*, Chicago, IL: Follett.

Knox, H and MacLennan, A (1994) *Coping with the Challenge of Growth: Proceedings of the Innovation 1994 Conference on Curriculum and Professional Development for Larger Numbers in Higher Education*, Bangor.

Koberg, D and Bagnall, J (1991) *The Universal Traveller*, Menlo Park, CA: Crisp Publications.

Kolb, DA (1984) *Experiential Learning*, New York: Prentice-Hall.

Laurillard, D (1993) *Rethinking University Teaching: A framework for the effective use of educational technology*, London: Routledge.

Leiblum, MD (1992) 'Implementing CAL at a university', *Computers in Education*, 18, 109–18.

Lessem, R (1984) 'The gestalt of action learning', in Cox, C and Beck, J (eds) *Management Development - Advances in practice and theory*, Chichester: Wiley.

Liston, DP and Zeichner, KM (1991) *Teacher Education and the Social Conditions of Schooling*, London: Routledge, Chapman and Hall.

Little, P and Ryan, G (1991) 'Innovation in a nursing curriculum: a process of change', in Boud, D and Feletti, G (eds) *The Challenge of Problem-based Learning*, London: Kogan Page.

McGill, I, Segal-Horn, S, Bourner, T and Frost, P (1976) 'Action learning: a vehicle for personal and group experiential learning', in Cooper, CL (ed.) *Theories of Group Processes*, Chichester: Wiley.

MacLennan, A (1995) 'Institutional Policy (1): the University of Paisley', in Raban, C and MacLennan, A (eds) *CATS in Context: putting principles into practice*, Sheffield: Pavic Publications.

Marton, F and Saljo, R (1984) 'Approaches to learning', in Marton, F *et al.* (eds) *The Experience of Learning*, Edinburgh: Scottish Academic Press.

Maurer, H, Kappe, F, Sherbakov, N and Srinivasan, P (1993) 'Structured browsing of hypermedia databases', *Proceedings of VCHCI '93*, Vienna, Austria: Springer, LNCS 733.

Middlehurst, R (1993) *Leading Academics*, Buckingham: Society for Research into Higher Education and the Open University Press.

Moore, GT (1991), 'Initiating problem-based learning at Harvard Medical School', in Boud, D and Feletti, G (eds) *The Challenge of Problem-based Learning*, London: Kogan Page.

National Board of Employment, Education and Training (NBEET) (1992) *Skills Required of Graduates: One test of quality in Australian higher education*, Canberra: Australian Government Publishing Service. (Also referred to as *Skills Sought by Employers of Graduates* on front cover of published report).

Newberg, L, Rouse, R and Kruper, J (1995) 'Integrating the World-Wide Web and multi-user domains to support advanced network-based learning environments', in *Proceedings of ed.-Media 95*, 494–9.

Nicholson, A (1994) 'The MSc in information technology and learning at Lancaster University: a student perspective', *CTISS file*, 17, 20–22.

Nott, M, Riddle, M and Pearce, J (1995) 'Enhancing traditional university science teaching using the World Wide Web', *Proceedings of the VI World Conference on Computers in Education (WCCE '95)*, London: Chapman and Hall.

O'Reilly, D (1993) 'Negotiating in an institutional context', in Stephenson, J and Laycock, M (eds) *Using Learning Contracts in Higher Education*, London: Kogan Page.

Pascarella, ET and Terenzini, PT (1991) *How College Affects Students*, San Francisco, CA: Jossey Bass.

Pascarella, ET *et al.* (1994) *What have we Learned from the First Year of the National Study of Student Learning?*, Pennsylvania, PA: National Center on Postsecondary Teaching, Learning and Assessment.

Pask, G (1988) 'Learning strategies, teaching strategies, and conceptual or learning style', in Schmeck, RR (ed.) *Learning Strategies and Learning Style*, New York: Plenum Press.

Pearce J, Ferguson, S and Spalding, B (1992) 'Letter from a student: syndicate learning and the student teacher', *New Era in Education*, 73, 38–41.

Percy, K and Ramsden, P (1980), *Independent Study: Two examples from English higher education*, Guildford: Society for Research into Higher Education.

Perret-Clermont, A (1980) *Social Interaction and Cognitive Development in Children*, London: Academic Press.

Perry, WG (1970) *Forms of Intellectual and Ethical Development in the College Years*, New York: Holt Rinehart Winston.

Perry, WG (1988) 'Different worlds in the same classroom', in Ramsden, P (ed.) *Improving Learning: New perspectives*, London: Kogan Page.

Peters, T (1992) *Liberation Management: Necessary disorganisation for the nanosecond nineties*, London: BCA.

Phillips-Kerr, B, (1991) *A Survey of Careers Destinations: 1985 Modern Language Graduates of the Universities of Bradford, Hull, Newcastle Upon Tyne, Sheffield and the Polytechnic of Newcastle Upon Tyne*, Newcastle: University of Newcastle Careers Advisory Service.

Rainer, T (1980) *The New Diary*, London: Angus and Robertson.

Ramsden, P (1991) 'A performance indicator of teaching quality in higher education: the Course Experience Questionnaire', *Studies in Higher Education*, 16, 2, 129–50.

Ramsden, P (1992) *Learning to Teach in Higher Education*, London: Routledge.

Robertson, D (1994) *Choosing to Change: Extending access, choice and mobility in higher education*, London: Higher Education Quality Council.

Sangster, A (1995) 'World Wide Web – what can it do for education?', *Active Learning*, 2, 3–8.

Schön, DA (1984) 'The architectural studio as an example of education for reflection-in-action', *Journal of Architectural Education*, 38, 2–9.

Schwartz, PL, Heath, CJ and Egan, AG (1994) *The Art of the Possible: Ideas from a traditional medical school engaged in curricular revisions*, Dunedin, New Zealand: University of Otago Press.

Shlechter, TM, (1991) `What do we really know about small group CBL?', paper presented at the Annual Conference of the Association for the Development of Computer-based, Instructional Systems, St Louis.

Steeples, C (1995a) 'Computer mediated collaborative writing in higher education: enriched communication support using voice annotations', in *Proceedings of the World Conference on Computers in Education (WCCE 95)*, London: Chapman and Hall.

Steeples, C (1995b) 'Educational models for computer conferencing', *CTI Newsletter: Centre for Land Use and Environmental Sciences*, 15, 3.

Steeples, C, Goodyear, P and Mellar, H (1994) 'Flexible learning in higher education: the use of computer-mediated communications', *Computers and Education*, 22, 1/2, 83–90.

Steeples, C, Shapiro, JJ and Hughes, S (1995) 'Promoting dynamic learning communities: computer-mediated communications (CMC) as agents for cultural change', *Proceedings of the International Conference on Computers in Education (ICCE 95)*, Singapore.

Stephenson, J (1988) 'The experience of independent study at North East London Polytechnic', in Boud, D (ed.) *Developing Student Autonomy in Learning (2nd edn)* London: Kogan Page.

Stephenson, J (1993) 'The student experience of independent study', in Graves, N *Learner Managed Learning*, Leeds: Higher Education for Capability.

Stephenson, J and Laycock, M (eds) (1993) *Using Learning Contracts in Higher Education*, London: Kogan Page.

Stott, D (1992) *Student-centred Learning*, London: Council for National Academic Awards.

Telford, A (1995) 'Mixed-mode delivery: the best of both worlds?', in Thomas, D (ed.) *Flexible Learning Strategies in Higher and Further Education*, London: Cassell.

Thomas, P (1986) *'The structures and stability of learning approaches'*, unpublished PhD thesis, University of Queensland.

TLTP (1993) 'Teaching and Learning Technology Projects: TLTP', *The CTISS File*, 15, 27–70.

TLTP II (1993) 'Teaching and Learning Technology Programme: Phase II', *The CTISS File*, 16, 6–7.

Tomlinson, P and Saunders, S (1995) 'The current possibilities for teacher profiling in teacher education', in Edwards, A and Knight, P (eds) *The Assessment of Competence in Higher Education*, London: Kogan Page.

Torbert, WR (1978) 'Educating toward shared purpose, self-direction and quality work: the theory and practice of liberating structure', *Journal of Higher Education*, 49, 2, 109–35.

Trigwell, K (1995) 'Increasing faculty understanding of teaching', in Wright, WA and associates (eds) *Teaching Improvement Practices*, Bolton, MA: Anker.

Trigwell, K and Prosser, M (1991) 'Improving the quality of student learning: the influence of learning context and student approaches to learning on learning outcomes', *Higher Education*, 22, 251–66.

Trigwell, K, Prosser, M and Taylor, P (1994) 'Qualitative differences in approaches to teaching first year university science', *Higher Education*, 27, 75–84.

Tuckman, BW (1965) 'Developmental sequence in small groups', *Psychological Bulletin*, 63, 6, 384–99.

Vermunt, JDHM (1989) *'The interplay between internal and external regulation of learning, and the design of process-oriented instruction'*, paper presented at the Third Conference of the European Association for Research on Learning and Instruction, Madrid.

Weil, SW and McGill, I (1989) 'A framework for making sense of experiential learning', in Weil, SW and McGill, I (eds) *Making Sense of Experiential Learning*, Buckingham: Society for Research into Higher Education and the Open University Press.

Wheeler, S and Birtle, J (1993) *A Handbook for Personal Tutors*, Buckingham: Society for Research into Higher Education and the Open University Press.

Winter, R (1995) 'The assessment of professional competences: the importance of general criteria', in Edwards, A and Knight, P (eds) *The Assessment of Competence in Higher Education*, London: Kogan Page.

Zeichner, KM and Teitelbaum, K (1982) 'Personalised and enquiry-oriented teacher education: an analysis of two approaches to the development of curriculum for field-based experiences', *Journal of Education for Teaching*, 8, 2, 95–117.

Zimmerman, BJ (1989) 'Models of self-regulated learning', in Zimmerman, BJ and Schunk, DH (eds) *Self-regulated Learning and Academic Achievement*, New York: Springer-Verlag.

Zimmerman, BJ (1990) 'Self-regulated learning and academic achievement: an overview', *Educational Psychologist*, 25, 1, 3–17.

Index